HOW TO WEEP IN PUBLIC

HOW
TO
WEEP
IN
PUBLIC

··

FEEBLE OFFERINGS ON DEPRESSION
FROM ONE WHO KNOWS

··

JACQUELINE NOVAK

THREE RIVERS PRESS
NEW YORK

Published in the United States by Three Rivers Press, an imprint
of the Crown Publishing Group, a division of Penguin Random
House LLC, New York.
www.crownpublishing.com

Three Rivers Press and Tugboat design are registered trademarks
of Penguin Random House LLC.

Library of Congress Cataloging-in-Publication Data
Names: Novak, Jacqueline.
Title: How to weep in public : feeble offerings on depression from
    one who knows / Jacqueline Novak.
Description: New York : Three Rivers Press, 2016.
Identifiers: LCCN 2015041925 (print) | LCCN 2015045864
    (ebook) | ISBN 9780804139700 (paperback) |
    ISBN 9780804139717 (ebook)
Subjects: LCSH: Novak, Jacqueline. | Comedians—United
    States—Biography. | Depression, Mental—Humor. | BISAC:
    HUMOR / Form / Parodies. | HUMOR / Topic / Adult. |
    BIOGRAPHY & AUTOBIOGRAPHY / Personal Memoirs.
Classification: LCC PN2287.N577 A3 2016 (print) | LCC
    PN2287.N577 (ebook) | DDC 818/.602—dc23
LC record available at http://lccn.loc.gov/2015041925

ISBN 978-0-8041-3970-0
eBook ISBN 978-0-8041-3971-7

Printed in the United States of America

Cover design by Christopher Brand
Cover photograph by George Baier IV

10 9 8 7 6 5 4 3 2 1

First Edition

For the depressos

CONTENTS

PART TWO: HOW TO CULTIVATE YOUR DEPRESSION AS A YOUNG ADULT 83

INTRODUCTION:
HOW TO WEEP IN PUBLIC

People often talk wistfully about the rapid passing of time. "If only you could hit pause on life," they sigh, as if "pausing" were but a magical notion. But the depressed know pause is possible, and we *achieve* it. We pull our boats out of the water, ensuring that even as the river of time continues to roll along, we'll make no real progress.

Whether you are very depressed or only a little, or not at all (so you *think*), you deserve a break from the ever-gushing deluge. I know how it is. Life can feel like a never-ending game of tag. To that I say: Let this book be your base. Catch your breath here, friend. Take a moment. You can pretend to read it if you like. Or just hug it like a teddy bear. Hugging a book looks collegiate, not childish, so you will be safe from prying eyes and maybe even attract the attention of a roaming professor looking to take advantage.

Think of this book as your pause button. Make yourself at home inside its pages. Rest assured, I won't try to push anything on you—no probing questions or helpful exercises. I *definitely* won't try to cure you. Why? Because I'm still pretty depressed myself, and "trying" isn't exactly one of my hobbies at the moment. I'll just keep you company for a little while. Nothing more, nothing less. No false promises of a life free of depression here—you can count on that.

But what if you're not up to reading a book in your condition? What if you're still waiting for your new meds to kick in? I get it. Hauling your focus left to right through the muck of a sentence, back to the left, and down a level—only to start the trudge through a new line—can feel less like a leisure pursuit and more like natural-resistance strength training.

Look, however you decide to hobble along for this ride (or not) is fine with me. Feel free to skim, start at the end, or each morning open to an arbitrary page as if you're pulling a tarot card. Enjoy the book while curled on the floor in a fetal position . . . after all, that's how I wrote it. I'm just giddy you're here at all.

Please understand I use the word *giddy* in the way Helen Keller used the word *see*—that is, relative to my own experience, because at the moment, much like you, I feel almost completely numb to an already narrowed emotional spectrum. Know that I use words with traditionally positive connotations only as a sort of shorthand. Language will fail us in many ways throughout these pages. But we must plug away at the cause.

The limitations of language have been ruining my life for a long time. Once I told a guy I was a "bleeding-heart liberal" for him. I meant I just couldn't help loving him, but it came off as a political statement. For a while, I also thought *heroine* was just a fancier word for *hero*, so I told another guy he reminded me of a Victorian-era heroine. I guess the real problem is that I need to stop complimenting guys.

No matter how good you are with words, it's inevitable that meaning is lost between your mind and someone else's. Trying to communicate is like chucking a cup of water at a thirsty person's face. It's better than nothing, sure, and a teaspoon of water might hit their lips, but oh, God, there's just *so* much water in the grass.

I've tried to use sex in place of language, but no one yet has been capable of processing the imagery, references, and metaphors I imbue into my thrusts, so I've returned to common English.

Yes, this book will be made up of words and sentences, bound to misrepresent me. But at least there will be no outright promises of help. No pressure or appeals to buck up, and not a single skyward tug on a bootstrap. Again, I'm just here to keep you company while you waste away in the prison cell of your mood. I'm like that guard who provided Saddam Hussein with Doritos during the days leading up to Hussein's execution.

Think of it this way: while most books on depression try to help you win the war, this one is merely a cigarette in the trenches. Truthfully, with your feet blistering and boots wet, you are not in a place to combat your mood anyway. So you can sit there and continue to shit yourself or you can accept a bit of comfort from a fellow soldier.

Go ahead and take this hit of nicotine. Make yourself cozy. The war on your mood disorder can wait. By simply sitting inside your depression, by giving in to it rather than trying to fight it, you have achieved something momentous, something enviable . . . don't let anyone tell you otherwise.

Most people can't stand to let things be awful, so they instigate some drama. They fuck someone's aunt, withhold someone's pension, or refuse to validate your parking ticket, based entirely on the fact that they dislike your ascot.

But you? You may be slumped on your carpet, but for that, my friend, you are a radical. You have dared to hit pause, and now you are just sitting there inside the pause, floating in space like Neil Armstrong. In your own weak way, you are one of the heroic explorers of our time.

You might be thinking, *Hmm, I don't feel proud.*

Well, then, outsource your self-esteem to me, and let me be proud on your behalf. By not even pretending to be a person and, instead, scurrying away from your responsibilities, you are willing to go where others aren't. You are bold. You are brave.

But what if you are too depressed to buy in to your own weasel-like courage, you ask? I get that. But really, what else are you going to read? *Best American Travel Writing?* Pretty much every book but this one risks bumming you out with the glittering details of a world you're incapable of experiencing. Since this book will speak *only* of the depressed life, it will keep you inside familiar territory and therefore be nonabrasive to your psyche.

This book is your chance to lean into your depression, to firm up the depressed habits you already possess, while adding a wonderful array of freshly disturbing, unpleasant symptoms and behaviors to your repertoire—a richer variety of grays to your already gray landscape.

But what if your world isn't gray, you ask? What if you're not depressed at all? Well, chances are you will be. Depression is extremely common and only becoming more so every day. Did you know that one in five people experiences major depressive episodes before dying? And with humans living longer, those numbers are probably headed the way of the herpes ratio. Long story short: it's almost guaranteed you're going to happen into an episode of major depression before you die.

Which reminds me . . . we're all going to die, and I don't mean that in a platitudinous way. I mean to insert in your mind's eye the graphic visual of your croaking out your last rattler of an exhale. Best-case scenario, you'll die in a beige room, on top of Plasticine sheets, surrounded by your "loved ones"—a grotesque euphemism for family members who'll flaunt the most heinous accoutrements of their personalities for weeks on end with an indignant "I'm in *mourning!*"

How are you feeling now? Have I nudged you any closer to a depression? If you are concerned you are immune but yearning to explore these intriguing waters, I say let this book be your entry point. I'm confident that if you remain open minded, you might just slip into a serendipitous depression of your own when you least expect it.

I'm here to help you explore the wild world of the depressed life and make the most of your depression, by which I mean suffer its many facets in full. After all, if you're gonna do something, you might as well do it all the way.

Well, not *all the way*.

I'd like to state now that in order to lead a depression-rich life, you must remain alive. If you're having suicidal thoughts, I do want to gently commend you, because technically you're on the right track. But you must put on the brakes.

In order to experience depression in its most potent form you want to take it to its limit, but not its (un)natural conclusion. Think of it like Tantric sex. Tantric masters cultivate their internal energy through sexual activity and then, instead of ejaculating on climax, retain their semen and enjoy the unclear benefits. You, too, must not let your depression "climax."

This is the National Suicide Prevention Lifeline number: 1-800-273-8255.

Again, I don't want you to go over the edge, but I do encourage you to behave recklessly with your own psyche. A good rule of thumb: never avoid horrific thoughts, otherwise known as the Truth.

Maybe it's true that being a free and loose thinker

leads you to wastelands where meaning breaks down and depression erects a corrupt makeshift government. But if that's the case, I still say, good. Go there. *At all costs.* Most Americans never see Paris, and you're gonna tell them to also limit their mental universe? Is there a more horrifying restriction? Expanding your mind has to be a good thing, right?

It's not like people who constantly repress their dark thoughts escape depression. They end up on the floor anyway. And your depression will be a much more interesting depression than that of the puritan who keeps a corset and bonnet on her thoughts.

Repressors spend their lives making up fictions, shoving down ideas, and threatening to bury them, like: *When Papa lifts my skirts in the barn, maybe it's not actually an old farming technique to help the cows get in the mood to be milked . . . ? Nah, best trust Papa.*

Now, in that scenario, nobody's happy. Papa is, we hope, ashamed. The girl is depressed but doesn't know why. And Nellie, the cow, is suffering a grand depression, too, because (a) she lived as a milk machine, and (b) she did "go there," let herself know the truth, that she lived in a house of violent incest and lies. I'd rather be Nellie. Wouldn't you?

It was this realization that inspired the book you are now reading. I was in a dark place at the time: my parents' house, which stands in the shade of too many glorious maples. I'd recently been inexplicably fired from a Manhattan advertising agency job after I stopped showing up. With no job, I opted not to renew my lease and instead took a train to my parents' house in the sub-urbs, telling them I needed to shore up and get better.

At some point, I set out (read: rolled over in the direction of my laptop) to write. I had been lying in bed reading self-help books and started to notice that they were all by people who were either "completely cured" or nonsufferers. And suddenly: *Eureka!* I figured that even if what I wrote was depressing, narrow, or dull, someone out there might enjoy taking a break from being lectured at to relax in the company of somebody who gets it.

Five years later, I guess I am doing "better," but one never really knows. I attribute this general better-ness to a combination of meds and my shifting program of questionable practices, like sleeping with crystals under my pillow and switching to the drug Lamictal.

But the depression isn't gone. Part of doing better is learning *not* to freak out every time I feel depression nudging its boner against my backside.*

Doing better doesn't mean I'm cured, but it does mean I've learned how to be "better" at being depressed. I've accumulated skills that can only come from years of experience, and it is from this subterranean vantage point—as an expert at mental (un)health—that I am now talking to you, my readers.

---

* Crass, sexual metaphors will be used liberally throughout the book to lighten the mood, but you will get used to it. And if you think that's cheap, let me remind you that so are caramels, and they are delicious.

Think of this book as a little promise that somewhere, someone—namely me—approves of you, even in your lowliest state. This book is me saying to you, "It's cool."

WHAT THIS BOOK WILL NOT PROVIDE:

- Useful exercises
- Insights of lasting value
- Relief from depression
- Help of any kind

WHAT THIS BOOK WILL PROVIDE:

- Mild entertainment for the immobilized depressive when cable/Internet's out
- Feeling of being ever-so-slightly less alone before loneliness returns even stronger
- "Fun" activities to occupy the mind during its travels through hell
- Small book-shaped headrest

Got it? Okay, so let's do this thing!

Sorry.

I don't mean to sound like a red-faced, silver-haired football coach croaking out commands.

Really I'm talking to myself anyway, more like if Coach were quietly encouraging his flaccid penis to do him proud.

So what I mean to say is:

Me, do this thing!

You, just relax.

....

PART ONE

HOW TO BE A DEPRESSIVE-IN-TRAINING AS A CHILD

....

Most people pace their soul-searching over the course of a lifetime, grappling with the suffering of the human condition when events inspire it.

Resist this willy-nilly approach and dive face-first into the darkness *as a child*! Leap at it like it's a Slip 'N Slide, with enthusiasm and a running start, despite knowing there are rocks in the grass and that pain is inevitable. *Welcome it*.

Think of it as burning through the coursework of human pain and struggle—from Angst 101 to Advanced Anguish—before you even reach puberty. Plant the seed early so that when depression strikes later in life *no one* will be surprised.

Luckily, childhood offers no shortage of suffering, even if you're born into a comfortable life, and even if you're not an overly sensitive pre-depresso like I was. Life is a rude awakening for everyone. You go from a nice warm womb to an overwhelming world of stimuli and strange people. It's a lot to deal with ... hence all the shrieking kids. Even in a place as airy as Target, a kid will whiz by as a passenger in a fun red cart and yell as if to the mountains. As I try on some Mossimo flats, I'll nod to myself, as if the child were a clever colleague who'd just made an excellent point. In response to most babies' wailing, I find myself thinking, *Indeed.*

I realize that if you're reading this you're probably no longer a child yourself, so it may be too late for you to heed this advice, but please consider passing it along to a young niece or nephew.

To all you kids, if you're not sure where to start, let me give you a hint. Simply take some time from playing with others to sit alone in the dark of a closet or under a stairwell and think about how one day your parents will croak. Not just in a general way. I want you to consider the following: even if all goes ideally, and your mom and dad don't die for a very, very long time, that is still a finite number of days you have left with them. And however many minutes there are between today and the day they die, those minutes are dropping away, literally by the minute.

Yes, the death of your parents is coming for you, slowly, maybe, but it's on its way. You can try to forget about it, and you will, but in those happy times of forgetting, the minutes are still steadily ticking. They say the watched pot never boils. But if you look away, you may soon hear the sputter and shriek of your sister telling you Dad's heart has failed.

I'm not trying to bum you out, I'm just helping you digest this painful truth now, when you are better equipped and haven't yet learned a thousand methods to rationalize away the simple, painful image of matching His and Her coffins in your parents' preferred wood stain.

Getting comfortable with these ideas now allows you to lead a more rich mental life—more vividly dark and disturbing, that is—as an adult depressive later. You don't want to be forty, suffering a depressive attack, and weeping over the suddenly obvious realization that your parents, if not already dead, are mortal.

You want your agony to have a certain sophistication, no? You don't want people to think you're some simpleton who just suddenly realized life is hard, do you? Well, then, first you need to build a solid foundation, and that is what the following chapters are all about: bringing out the little turtlenecked French nihilist in you as a child. You need to cultivate your neuroses. Even if you only have one mental breakdown later in life, this early work will make it easier for you to "lose it" with gusto when the time is right.

And don't feel like you've missed out if you're already a full-grown adult depressive. This means you probably did excellent work as a child, and that's something to celebrate. Better yet, you still have the fun ahead of searching desperately through your past for your depresso-origin story, the missing link that will explain all, a mythos to match your pathos.

....

CHAPTER ONE

BABYHOOD:
EARLY PRACTICE IN CRYING WHILE MAKING EYE CONTACT WITH STRANGERS

As early as possible, preferably when you're still swaddled in a hospital blanket, you'll want to telegraph an inherent weakness to a parent, guardian, or stern orphanage matron. It plants a seed so that when you slip into your first significant breakdown, they don't pass it off as healthy ol' you becoming melodramatic.

More than likely, you *are* a completely healthy, happy kid. Even if you're struggling a bit, there's no way you're *really* legitimately depressed as a baby. It's not possible. In truth, you are a little ball of dough in the oven, changing form so rapidly that it would be rude for anyone to make assessments. Parents, stop opening the oven door! Let them bake and get glacially cool before tasting.

But setting a certain tone as a baby can soften the blow of your eventual depression. You want them thinking, *Ah, I always knew she had a melancholic streak!* or, depending on their worldview, *That child was marked, ever since great-great-great-grandmother Henrietta made the deal with the Hooved One.*

Whatever the case, you should tip 'em off early. If you wait to suggest you have an ill-functioning brain until, say, the age of five, those in charge might just blame it on the stresses of kindergarten.

No, what you want is family members nodding over their mugs of rooibos in the next room, stage-whispering comments like, "Well, I saw this coming since the day you brought her home. If you took her blankie away, she wouldn't cry, she'd just roll her stroller as fast as she could into the nearest wall."

Okay, that might be a bit theatrical, but you know your audience better than I do.

If my audience, my mom, is to be believed, my own performance must have been Oscar worthy. Even as a newborn in the hospital, I tended to turn away and bury my face. Disturbing, isn't it? How sad to imagine a baby taking her first few sniffs of Life on Earth and deciding this place just isn't for her.

But I have to admit, it *does* sound like me. Why angle my face toward the harsh sensory input of the world when a simple adjustment of the head could plant it in some soft crib lining. Can babies even turn their heads? Maybe that's what made my resistance to the world so remarkable: the fact that I wanted it so bad I learned to work my neck muscles on day one.

My mom also tells me I was born "cold." Sounds vampiric, but no such luck. I wonder if I was only playing possum, making myself cold on purpose, willing my core temperature to drop, Tibetan monk–like, believing that if they thought me nonviable, they'd cover my face with a sheet and leave me be.

Faking one's death would've been a selfish ruse for my wrinkly self to pull, but one can surely understand a newborn just wanting to be left alone for five minutes, to gather her thoughts and drum up some nerve without the expectant parental gaze.

Whatever I was up to, my ruse didn't work; the nurses did not ferry me to the morgue. Instead, they noticed I was a bit chilly, so they gave me a hat and mittens.

My mom smiles at the memory of me in hat and mittens. Apparently, this is meant to be a cute story, but cuteness has a dark underbelly, especially when you ask yourself why people delight in a newborn in a hat, a Chihuahua wearing a raincoat, or even a teakettle wearing a knit cozy. I suspect it amuses us to see a creature whom we (rudely) perceive as possessing a lower consciousness appear to have chosen to adorn itself, as if it had agency, when we know the truth: the little being is completely, helplessly under our control.

But that's an issue for another day. The question that needs to be asked now is how *long* did it take for the nurses to notice my temperature was low and find me a hat? It's not like they keep a basket of tiny ski caps in every linen closet. Oh yes, I was born in a linen supply closet at a North Carolina hospital because all the birthing rooms were full.

Why was the birthing ward so crowded? I can't

answer that, other than to theorize that apparently nine months earlier, my mom was not the only woman in NC who felt a little frisky after watching Gregory Peck on TV, and then proceeded to initiate an encounter without a prophylactic. According to my parents, it was quite the scene at the hospital: a long line of globular women on beds, legs bent and wide, snaking through the hallway, and probably out to the parking lot.

I wonder if the memory of that linen closet is buried deep in my subconscious. Did that less-than-glamorous location make me feel "less than" from the start? Maybe I entered the world with outrageous confidence, eyes closed with bliss, floating onto the stage like a grande dame in the arms of a few tuxedoed dancer boys, in this case my mom, the OB/GYN, and any nurses, who, having delivered me, I waved off to get out of my spotlight. Then, just as I was about to blow the roof off the place with my rendition of this ole ditty called Life, I opened my eyes and saw not the elaborate hospital room stage set I'd imagined . . . but a linen closet, a place where nurse practitioners abscond to fondle each other, where the occasional criminal changes into scrubs to pass himself off as a doctor.

Was it that first minute of my life that did me in, establishing a damaging precedent for my future self-talk? *Fold me and tuck me between some towels, life. Like a washcloth on the bottom shelf, I shall exist as a possibility for future use, but not for today.*

If it wasn't the linen closet that did me in, it must

have been the chill. Could it be that all my subsequent depression was caused by one of these minor facts? Or was it the perfect storm of all of them?

The idea that I've been psychologically fucking freezing since my first minutes of existence isn't the kind of thing I go around telling anyone except you. I realize it sounds a bit dramatic. With all the legitimate suffering out there, this girl thinks she's broken because she went without a hat for a few seconds?

The more I think about it, the more it makes sense. As an adult, whenever I have been at my most depressed, the cold is completely intolerable. Sometimes when the shower water isn't hot enough to steam the room in the morning, the suffering feels so intense that I'll pause to marvel at just how much weaker I am than other people. I might use my finger to just jot *weak* in the steam on the glass shower door, as a reminder to assess this fault some more the following day.

When I can't postpone it any longer and it's time to step out of the shower ... oh, God. I'll wrap a towel around my hunched-up shoulders like a short cape and walk stiffly through the apartment, moving slowly so the air doesn't fly at me too fast. Exposed from the waist down, I stalk past my boyfriend (yes, I have one now; more on that shortly) and back to bed for warmth. Sometimes I'll close my eyes and when asked why I'm going back to sleep, I explain that I'm doing no such thing: "My eyeballs are cold and I'm warming them up with my lids."

I know. It sounds so indulgent. If everyone let themselves be so pitifully pained by such minor discomforts, there would be no workforce. But this is how it is when you're depressed. The effects are truly outrageous—that's why they can bring a moderately intelligent person to a point where she honestly believes her depression genes were activated by a momentary lack of a beret.

Got that? I'll staunchly declare it's not that I'm a self-absorbed asshole for entertaining these seemingly far-fetched theories. It's the depression: it makes you desperate for answers. (Okay, I am also surely a "self-absorbed asshole," but for other reasons ... which I might enumerate for you over a three-course meal before thinking to say, "And how are you?")*

Keep in mind, these aren't the kind of thoughts you have on a bad day, or even a few weeks into a hearty first depression. No, these are the thoughts when the depression has been at you so long that you've already endlessly discussed all the appropriate questions about thyroid levels; you've listened to all the advice from therapists who tell you to "consider a hobby"; and you no longer

---

* While we're at it, let me divulge another thought that my depression has led me to entertain. I've wondered, in seriousness, if my use of a Ouija board during puberty—a time of constitutional change that I've read can make one vulnerable to negative energies—allowed some lower vibrational hellions to attach themselves to me, sucking the (limited) life force out of me ever since, and straight from the orifices, no doubt. I am referring to *spiritual* orifices, of course, the chakras.

introduce depression as a subject because it has become the universal context to *all* conversations.

I used to say to my parents, "Regarding my depression . . . ," before dumping on them my latest depression hypothesis. Now I'll just posit questions out of nowhere, because I trust that they know why I'm asking: "Do you think I might have a demon attached to me? Does my right eye look more dead than my left?"

Depression is confusing, and it becomes attractive to look for signs of its inevitability. Some might say this is a misplaced impulse, but I say, *go for it*. A bit of personal mythologizing makes things vastly more interesting when you're slogging through what the doctors say is a blatantly pathological brain state no more meaningful than bursitis. And since science hasn't really figured out depression, it's still a possibility that the demons, the hat, the linen closet are *all* to blame.

So if you've been struggling to understand your depression, sticking dutifully to reason so far, instead try pursuing these lines of thought no matter how crazy they may seem. I give you permission. Sure, you may have missed your chance to leave a breadcrumb trail of depressive foreshadowing moments, but it's never too late to invent hypothetical past infant traumas for yourself.

About the boyfriend, yes, at the time of this writing I have managed to secure a loving live-in suitor, but please don't take that to mean I'm now immune to depression.

Having a boyfriend can sometimes give others a false sense of your wellness and fool them into thinking you're doing better. They say to themselves, "She was merely in want of a good man." In some towns, being female and unloved is grounds to lock you up in a mental ward or in some cases administer euthanasia.

When I go to a restaurant on my own and the waiter removes the second place setting and calmly heads back to the kitchen, I half expect he's jumping on the phone to call the nearest Two Doves Convalescent Home for the Deranged and Hell-Bound.

I may have hooked a fellow, but I still have most of the same depressed habits: I lead a pantsless life, maintain a fourteen-hours-a-night sleep habit, and am unable to show up to any event that doesn't promise unlimited yet high-quality food. Any psychiatrist worth his Nepalese masks would say I suffer from, at the very least, an evergreen mood disorder.

Tonight, as I walked the city with this boyfriend, we landed at a chain barbecue restaurant. I ordered a frozen margarita. I've been drinking casually atop my meds for over a decade, and I'm certainly not going to stop now.

. . . .

TOP SIX WAYS TO RECAST YOUR CHILDHOOD AS ONE BIG LEAD-UP TO YOUR ADULT DEPRESSION

1. Find photos of yourself looking "out of it," and gaze at the pictures, sighing.
2. Look for people to blame, specifically teachers who may have shamed you. It's easy to find examples of adults making you feel less than . . . because you were.
3. Try to tease out a story from your parents or sibling about dropping you on your head.
4. Question your mother about what she fed you, and what nutrients you might have lacked.
5. Try to find a dirty, damaged stuffed animal and look upon it as a symbol of a broken childhood.
6. Anytime anyone recalls a positive memory from your childhood, mention "the tears of a clown when there's no one around."

. . . .

....

CHAPTER TWO

LET'S MAKE A FAMILY TREE:
WHERE EVERY FRUIT IS A MOOD DISORDER

If you want to feel confident in your eventual diagnosis of depression, attempt to find a family history of mental illness. Luckily, it's hard to come up empty in such a search. Maybe there's no evidence of genetic predisposition, but surely there's a heap of dysfunctional behavior passed from generation to generation that could do as much damage.

If you can't find evidence of a melancholic relative, don't worry . . . as I said earlier, *one in five* experiences a major depressive episode at some point in life. Whether the increase is due to chemicals in plastics, omega-3s not making it up the food chain, or EMF radiation of the hypothalamus, I'll leave to the scientists. Simply put, depression is your birthright as a human these days, regardless of your DNA.

As for me, family history suggests I possess both the

magic genes and the generations of dysfunctional behavior to support their expression. In the 1950s and '60s, my grandfather would drive three hours from Vermont to Albany to see a therapist. As a rabbi, he no doubt wanted to keep his emotional and psychological suffering a secret from his community. While most people today wouldn't trust a rabbi who *wasn't* in therapy, things were different back then, not to mention mostly in black and white.

It just wouldn't have inspired confidence in the congregants to know their leader was a tissue-plucking, ceiling-staring whimperer. Not a good look for a man of God: a supposed pillar of faith spending his off-hours weeping in the temple, forehead to the podium.

I only heard about Zaidie's moody past when I was well into my own depression in college. It might have been useful information to pick up earlier, but the fact that I believed myself predisposed for nothing but normalcy encouraged me to find my own unique route to depression. I didn't merely rely on legacy to get me in.

More important, if I'd been aware that depression was coming for me, I might have pursued some kind of health-and-happiness regimen to stave it off. Thankfully, I was ignorant, and so I was fearless. Not suspecting my genes might send a flood of craziness my way, I was never afraid to walk close to the water's edge.

Some people avoid darkness preemptively; I actively courted it. I was taught very early to not be afraid of thoughts, no matter how ugly. I received this lesson from both of my parents, because my dad—a pink-toned blue-eyed tall gentile—was a psych major in college and knew that repression is never the answer, and because my mom—an olive-skinned hazel-eyed Jewess—spent her own childhood afraid of her thoughts.

As a young girl, my mom was once seized by hysteria as she considered the fact that at any moment she could pull a knife from the drawer and stab herself. She wasn't tempted to self-harm; she was merely confronting the disturbing reality that nothing beyond willpower stands between us and horribly irreversible actions. You know, classic obsessive-compulsive disorder stuff.

But what did my grandparents say when she told them about this fear? They didn't say, "*Don't* worry!" or suggest the sound principle that since she didn't actually *want* to stab herself, she wouldn't, and should relax.

No, what they did was *hide the kitchen knives.*

Nowadays, my adult mother and father decry my grandparents' response as deeply dysfunctional, and it comes up as a kind of parable in our family. My parents assured me growing up that thoughts are different from actions. Just because you imagine doing something, doesn't mean you'll do it—an inversion of the success mantra "If you can conceive it, you can achieve it." I wasn't afraid.

I often imagine what it must have been like in my mom's childhood household. I think of my grandmother, scurrying around, gathering anything sharp, while my grandfather sits depressed, slumped in a chair in his study rereading Job. Did he think to mention the Knife Daughter to his secret therapist in Albany, I wonder?

He certainly didn't share it with friends. As leaders in their community, he and Gramma Mimi probably didn't share their problems with anyone. The expectation in their culture was that you'd handle your problems in the house, privately, like jackasses.

Okay, it's easy for me to hear this story and shake my head dismissively. It was a different time and place. And who knows what was really going on. Maybe Gramma Mimi had been suffering the same neuroses as her daughter, worrying about using one of the knives on herself. Perhaps when my mom voiced that same concern, she reacted like she did because it gave her an excuse to hide them from herself?

Amazingly, these dysfunctional dramas were, no doubt, interrupted by members of the congregation who would stroll up the street and knock on the metallic frame of my grandparents' screen door unannounced, seeking solace, advice—or at very least the calming presence of the rabbi, not to mention his wife, the rebbetzin, who could be counted on to serve up some of her famous sour cream cake, sliced with . . . a spoon.

I can sympathize with my grandparents, too, but I still feel mad on my mom's behalf. Who hasn't looked at a knife and become briefly entranced by what it could do if you lost your mind? It's the same thought people sometimes have when driving a car: *Wow, with one slight jerk of the steering wheel, I could go off the edge of this cliff.* It's a natural human instinct to have these thoughts. It doesn't mean you're going to do anything drastic.

And because no one freaked out when I had such thoughts, neither did I. But I took their attitude a step further, and became maybe too loose of a thinker . . . I know it's made me judgmental of people who actively keep certain doors closed in their minds—folks who say, "I don't go there," or refuse to enjoy the hilarious sexual violence in Todd Solondz films.

We already repress our unconscious thoughts. We know this from Freud, not to mention all those dicks accidentally animated into Disney films. Are we really going to start trying to push back the conscious ones, too?

I enjoy tossing around perverse thoughts, gasping, and realizing you come out unharmed. They're like those chunks of foam painted to look like rocks—fun to throw at people and watch them at first recoil, then realize they're fine. It's a great pastime.

Consider my cousins, who embrace the same loose, wild mindset that I do. They suffer the same family inheritance of anxiety, obsessive thinking, the works, but they neither run from it nor press it down—and no one hides the knives. If anything, we take out the knives, hold them to our necks, and laugh hysterically, saying, "It's so crazy! I could do it! I could do it!"

When we were growing up, we'd love nothing more than to play a grotesque game of Would You Rather, where we'd try to horrify one another by coming up with the most vile, sickening theoretical scenarios, such as, "If there was a gun to your head, would you rather (a) give Zaidie a blow job while he's tied up and unable to refuse or (b) write the words *dirty kikes* on his and Grandma Mimi's bedroom walls?" Of course, we'd stipulate that in either case, you would never be allowed to explain your actions to your cherished grandparents.

Some people would think we were merely young perverts, but I say we were doing something much more impressive and psychologically—dare I say—genius? We were creating less stress around thoughts. We were mocking them. By dredging up the most disgusting possible concepts, we were reminding ourselves that mental images can't actually hurt you. Talking about blowing Zaidie is just that, *talking.*

But talking is how we travel to the outer reaches of our mental landscape, outrageous places where we'd never want to live, but where we plant a few flags, so when truly paralyzing thoughts call us farther than we'd like to be from home, we find ourselves on turf we've already staked out as our own. *With this flag, upon which I've drawn a tasteless scene and inscribed an ugly sentiment, I claim this land of toothy beasts my home.*

....

CHAPTER THREE

PEDIATRIC HEALTH:
LEARNING TO SAY NO TO LIFE
WITH YOUR BODY

When I was around four or five, I had my yearly physical exam, in which I was ordered matter of factly by a nurse to provide a urine sample. Problem was, I hadn't realized urinating was on my itinerary, so I had peed before leaving the house. I told the nurse I just didn't have it in me.

She told me to sip some water from the water fountain and try again in a few minutes. I played along, but I knew that a fuller bladder wasn't going to be enough to overcome my now seized-up pubococcygeal muscle. I had shut down.

Eventually, hours later it seemed, they gave up and told my mom to take me home and just bring back a urine sample that afternoon. I was relieved, but as the day wore on, I still hadn't peed. Concerns grew, and my parents sat me on the carpeted landing on our entryway stairs, right by the bathroom, and handed me endless refills of water.

I remember other family members gathering to observe the spectacle. But for many years that followed, I had no memory of what happened next.

Then, a totally separate memory, or so I thought, popped up strangely in my head years later. It was disturbing enough that I felt compelled to ask about it but was pretty sure it was just a dream: an image of me, naked on my back on a table in a dark room, bright lights shining down on me, the silhouettes of female figures hovering over me . . . doing something to my vagina.

I wondered if the memory meant I'd been abducted by aliens and experimented upon by the Greys. But no, when I asked my mom, she admitted that what I had been remembering was my catheterization. They had stuck a tube up my urethra to get the urine out. It wasn't that there was anything physically wrong with me. But they had no choice. What were they supposed to do? The girl simply wasn't peeing.

Now that I know the whole story, it all makes sense. In later visits to the pediatrician's office, no one pressured me about peeing. They'd hand my mom a urine sample cup and tell us, in a notably overcasual way, to just bring one from home when we felt like it.

My guess is they changed their system thanks to me and learned not to put so much pressure on young children to pee. My revolt had been effective. My total shutdown had made a change, hopefully not just in our pediatrician's office but throughout the medical network, across our great nation.

Of course, I hadn't consciously acted out of a desire to help others. I had just been driven by my objection to pressure of any kind. It's an impulse I still *feel in me,* and depression has only strengthened it.

For example, when someone tries to tell me, "You need to sign this lease ASAP," I might not have the courage to say no, but I can be counted on to passive-aggressively refuse by willing myself into a state of psychosomatic blindness until they've retracted their request. Only after the landlord stops hounding me can he expect to see a signed document slide under his door.

You, too, are no doubt as capable.

If we depressos are going to use our skills for the greater good, we must be unwavering in our nonefforts. With nondepressed people, you see them all the time drumming up the energy to please people just to get 'em off their backs. We, on the other hand, stand firm in our resistance to pressure.

Our supposedly childish reactions to being asked to do something—panicking, running away, shutting down—are in fact our greatest strength. We are uniquely qualified to stand up against the stresses put upon us by those more capable. I think we alone could dismantle the tax system.

Take pride in your childish refusal. From nursery school on, I never responded well to pressure, and I'm glad I didn't. Frankly, if you are a child reading this, neither should you. While parents and teachers will regularly tell you to do this and that because "I say so" or because "life isn't fair" or any other three-word utterance meant to intimidate you, you should refuse.

Many children already react negatively to pressure, running and hiding when asked to clean a room, or being suddenly unable to sing the song they knew moments ago when having to present it to the class. If you want to lay the foundation for becoming a heroic adult depresso, the trick is to simply become an ace at childish refusals . . . and then *never* grow out of it.

What if you've already grown up and lost that ability to flop face-first onto a bed when you have to get dressed? Do not despair! You may be high functioning now, but you can turn this thing around.

Look deeply into your childhood to locate a memory of a total shutdown. Maybe you refused to eat breakfast when a tyrant tried to offer you an un-cinnamoned-and-sugared piece of toast. Perhaps you were told to put your crayons back in their box and instead you flushed them down the toilet. And then demanded the bigger box, with the sharpener on the back.

Once you uncover such a memory, let it serve as a touchstone. Let it give you strength (or all-encompassing weakness, really) whenever someone tries to pressure you into doing, frankly, anything.

And that is, of course, not an order.

....

CHAPTER FOUR

DEFINING MOMENTS:
ONE BIG TRAUMA OR
ONE MILLION INCIDENTAL ONES

Some of today's experts postulate—or "idiots claim," depending on your view—that depression comes from denying your emotions. Basically, an emotion overwhelms us, we classify it as unsafe, and because we don't let these feelings pass through, we become psychologically constipated, and all that backed-up shit causes our whole system to shut down (that is, depression).

In a lot of cases, it's some emotional biggie. You still haven't let yourself feel all that anger you have toward your mother for running off with a clown when your father was a perfectly respectable magician. A quality childhood trauma like that, followed by a swift refusal to really process your emotions, is an excellent way to ensure a depression later on.

Many of you may have arrived here today thanks to such terrific dissociative work as a youngster. To those of you who fall in this category, I salute you. But what about the young people who know depression is for them but have yet to enjoy any big traumas to use as a boost?

Luckily, there is a loophole for you kiddies who are stuck in a comfortable childhood, looking to make it happen. Freud said that the content of any repression is irrelevant; it's the repression itself that is the neurosis. This means that you could be repressing the most minor things, but by stuffing them down you're inviting them to turn into fetid weapons of self-obstruction.

In other words, maybe your future depression will be the result of a gazillion tiny unfelt childhood emotions. If you're already an adult reading this, you need to go through and painstakingly unrepress every baby shit fit you never had. It might be hard at first. You have to start with the easy stuff: the items bobbing near the surface of your consciousness.

You might not think of yourself in this way; you might believe you're not a repressor—but that's a classic sign of a repressor. It's supposed to be unconscious; that's the whole point. If you knew you were repressing an image of your neighbor Tristan's balls* trapped between his Jams shorts and the genital netting, it wouldn't be a true repression at all.

You might even be thinking, *Hey, that's not me, I totally remember glimpsing my neighbor Tristan's balls . . . he was doing scissor kicks on the beach.* But before you go patting yourself on the back for being a healthy nonrepressor, consider

---

* Maybe I should have titled this book *Tristan's Balls?*

this: maybe it's not the image of the balls that you're repressing but the feeling of *titillation* you experienced when you saw those very tangled genitals?

Some feel the only way to access truly repressed content and get your emotional colon humming again is to put yourself into intensive psychotherapy. But this is not twentieth-century Vienna or a Woody Allen film, and none of us has the cash. I'm confident you don't need analysis to prove that you're repressing. For all you know, you are one of the world's most brilliant repressors and *have no idea.*

I mean, how would you know? There are clues, of course, as Freud would tell us if he hadn't committed suicide. I know, I know, he had oral cancer, and hospice care wasn't what it is today. Technically it was euthanasia, administered by his physician per Freud's prior request, but it's only right to count that as a legit suicide. He'd no doubt interpret other people's self-destructive behavior as subconscious suicide, so I think his actual one deserves the title. At the very least, let's give him a taste of his own medicine and suggest that he brought about his own oral cancer as an expression of his vaginal hatred. (What is the mouth but a roomy, higher altitudinous vagina?)

The best way to figure out what you're repressing is to watch for leaks in the system, like when something seemingly small causes you to weep uncontrollably. I'm always delighted when this happens, assuming I'm about to strike a serious vein of emotional oil. I've never hit it big, "recovering" a hideous memory that explains it all. There are zero suspicious gaps in my memory, and I haven't been molested yet. Still, there are treasures to be found.

As an experiment, I recently attempted to dredge up and jot down as many memories as I could of little things that made me feel guilty or inexplicably sad, the stuff no one would think is even worth mentioning to a therapist. I hoped that while I wouldn't discover a cavern of golden brick traumas,* I might unrepress myself by locating one little tiny dirty coin at a time.

I decided to begin my journey with something that made me cry inexplicably: *The Karate Kid.* I hadn't seen the movie in years, but there I was sitting with my therapist when it all came back to me—the scene where the young protagonist, Daniel, kicks the bike his mother gave him and says, "Stupid bike."

I don't remember the exact circumstances from the movie, but I know Daniel had loved the bike and felt proud of it until suddenly, ashamed of not having a car, he hated it. Why did this affect me so? I tried to put it in the context of my own childhood micro-trauma. The therapist, meanwhile, sat rapt. This is the juicy stuff those clinicians live for. It was practically a recovered memory, even though it was just a scene from a movie. I think it counts.

She listened as I then shared a story from when I was

---

* Yes, I'm consumed with metaphors involving prospecting for oil, gold, really anything that'll get a man to leave his family and head west. It's surely a past-life thing.

five and an adult friend of my parents gave me a brace-let as a present. For some reason, I had told this family friend that I didn't like the bracelet, even though I then ended up wearing it every day for a year. It was a rainbow of big plastic heart-shaped beads. What's not to love? This lady must have felt so bad when I said I didn't like what she picked out for me. Why did I do that? Think-ing about it now, I could die. Worse, *she's* dead, so I can't even tell her.

But I could tell the therapist, and as soon as I did, the floodgates opened. In what must have been the most exciting stream of memories ever unloaded to her, I bravely confessed a lifetime of little repressed disap-pointments.

Most of them, unsurprisingly, had to do with my par-ents. For example, I admitted to the therapist how it still bummed me out that at a certain point in my childhood my mom and dad stopped putting out Easter eggs. Just because my older siblings were outgrowing the tradition, I deserved to be robbed of a childhood? Maybe that's why I insist on moving home all the time. To exact a pound of childhood out of 'em.

Then I told the therapist about my disappointment when my parents canceled our expensive swim member-ship, forcing me to rely on friends' guest passes to swim, an indignity that affects me to this day. Even recently, I've had nightmares about sneaking into Willowbrook. Ugh, what kind of person gets upset about stuff like this? I wasn't sure I could continue.

The therapist urged me on. In the interest of my health, I ended up confessing . . . one more thing. I was also . . . jealous of my cousin Rachel's Formica dresser and desk unit because it was the shiny kind, not matte like mine.

My stomach twisted in guilt as I said the words, guilt for not being grateful for the matte-finish Formica furniture my parents provided. By the end of our session, even though I was sobbing, I felt alive! The experience was cathartic.

Some find the unburdening of such innocuous micro-repressions embarrassing, like you're having major surgery on your large intestine and the nurse hands you a jar with a thousand tiny animal-shaped erasers you've swallowed over the years. But micro-repressions are real, and a great way for the trauma-free child to slowly but surely block her emotional colon.

If this sounds like you—if you haven't yet experienced any major youthful traumas—don't fear, by the time you're twenty, you'll be as emotionally stopped-up as the girl who brings home the class rabbit for Christmas vacation, only to have it chase and mount her house cat in an attempt to launch a cross-species breeding initiative.* As a micro-repressor, you can get so good at burying feelings that it becomes automatic, and then you do it all day long.

---

* This horror almost befell my family when I was in the fourth grade. Luckily, Snook the cat outran Snowball before he was able to show her the move he called the Nor'easter.

After my breakthrough at therapy, I started noticing myself doing micro-repression all the time. For example, whenever I see a dog that I don't find cute, I feel
so guilty that I don't even allow the words "not cute"
to enter my consciousness, but instead start convincing
myself it *is* cute. I just find it so sad to imagine the dog
knowing I don't think it's the cutest dog out there.

So now, as part of my brave healing work, I've been
trying to allow myself to think a dog isn't that cute. Or
at least, *my* kind of cute. Baby steps.

If you start to experiment with your feelings like
this, especially after a lifetime of repressing them, there
can be messy moments. A few years ago, I beat my mom
in Scrabble, and I experienced an unexpected joy that
shames me even now. We're not one of those earnest
Scrabble families, by the way. This wasn't "game night,"
when Pops makes his famous spelt pizzas or some nonsense. After reluctantly agreeing to play, I started racking
up astonishing numbers, requiring numerous additions
and multiplications per turn. I was simply annihilating
my mother.

What you must know is that she is a very nice woman
and was truly happy for me. But the pleasure I felt at
taking her down, it was unholy. I tried to hold it in at
first, my depressive default. But because of the new anti-
repression work, I suddenly became aware of my emotional clenching, and something in me chose to release.

Oh, God. As I sat there, before her soft, kind, mid-
sixties face and strange hands, I cackled like a witch. I
knew my display was rude, and I was disoriented by the

unexpected joy. So I started weeping, which felt so ridiculous that I started laughing more. Then *that* laughter inspired more sobbing.

It must have looked like an exorcism, but it was in its way another breakthrough. My mom tried to tell me, "It's okay to feel happy you're winning. It's *okayyyy*."

My dad walked into the kitchen and, not remotely surprised to see sobbing and laughing over the Scrabble game, just poured himself some seltzer and headed back to his home office.

Oh, Mom and Dad. The same nice pair who kept me free of major traumas as a child, now dutifully allowing me to work through the burden of creating my own— and playing along kindly as I tell them part of my new therapy involves actively expressing every emotion as it comes up. "You will just have to deal with the consequences," I tell them. And yes, it will happen *wherever* it needs to happen.

A few years ago, I had the lovely opportunity to go on a big family vacation *as an adult*. It was an expensive vacation, just the kind of thing to trigger my guilt. My dad paid for it out of very hard-earned money!

My father has always been a hard worker, but at that time the contrast couldn't have been starker: him working away in his office, even as he was nearing retirement age, because he could in no way count on me to one day take care of him and my mom. He is a generous man. And he probably thought it would help me to have sunlight actually touch my skin.

He was right. I was very much enjoying myself on the

beach and became especially excited after I heard that my mom and sister had made reservations for a "dolphin swim." For some reason, the image of me gliding along with a dolphin held some magical appeal, like I would *become one* with the great fish (I mean, mammal) and it would glide me right out of my depression.

Knowing the event was scheduled for a few days into the trip, I even hung out near the dolphin hut a bit, getting myself psyched up. But then I happened upon some laminated literature describing the different tiers of dolphin experience. There was "Swim with the Dolphins," "Water Visit," and "Beach Intro." I suddenly became very concerned. The water visit involved nothing more than a photo with a dolphin, standing next to him in . . . shallow water.

Let me be clear. Standing next to a dolphin isn't even a thing. A dolphin has no legs. Standing next to him is a meaningless act. There is absolutely no excuse for choosing Water Visit over Dolphin Swim. For almost a week, I had been dreaming of swimming with the slimy angels, imagining the soft arcing above the surface and below, cool and blue.

But now, I had been brought back to earth. "Water Visit," my mom confirmed. The woman said it as if it was of no import, ham sandwiches rather than turkey, no big deal. But to me it was a huge deal. I had created an elaborate fantasy of me and my family, looking like those *other families* I had seen, the ones in the glossy brochures. Now, I was feeling something hideous: the emotion known as "bummed."

To most, being bummed isn't such a bad feeling. It's one of the most obvious, simple everyday experiences. But not to me. The shame over feeling bummed, and the idea of my parents knowing I'm bummed . . . this, I cannot stomach. Stupid bike, ugly bracelet, embarrassing guest pass, unsatisfying water visit.

Seriously. I would feel more comfortable being overtaken by a sudden urge to stab an elderly lady (I mean, not my mom, a different elderly lady). As we know, I'm not afraid of knife-related thoughts. But this, it just sounds so spoiled: *A beautiful vacation isn't enough for me—I need more!* Like a red-faced toddler screaming for a new toy.

I certainly didn't want to feel that way. I tried to hide it. But my mom's radar is unstoppable. She turned to my dad, who was working on his laptop at that very moment (even on vacation, he was still toiling), and said, "Jacqueline's upset because she thought we were *swimming* with the dolphins." I quickly tried to shush her, not wanting Dad to think I was ungrateful.

"It's okay to feel disappointed," she offered.

No, it's not. It's horrible. For being this ungrateful, I *deserve* the Water Visit. I tried to be mature, to honor the therapy I'd been doing for some time by "making space" for my repellent disappointment, but to also attempt to make things right.

I solemnly drove my golf cart to the activities shack to see if there was any way I could tag along with another family's dolphin swim. At that point, I would have gone off with a family *for life* if it meant a chance to swim with a dolphin, but there were no spots left.

I remembered standing on the dry sand watching the dolphins from afar, wondering if I'd be able to summon the emotional strength to meet up later with my family for the Water Visit. I knew I was being ridiculous. If I really needed to swim with the dolphins so badly, I thought, I should probably look into becoming a marine biologist. My mom suggested the same thing later. Well, it was more in the context of getting a job.

The ending of the story is that I did find the courage to show up for the Water Visit (hidden reserves of bravery can surprise you), and I suppose I enjoyed myself. It could have been worse. It could have been the Beach Intro. That's for children scared of water. They lure the dolphins to the shore with some cod tenders and then you wave at them. It's like watching a video of a dolphin on YouTube.*

Okay, it may sound like I still haven't gotten over the experience, and maybe that's why I'm still talking about it . . . to make sure I don't repress the feelings and have to pay to uncover them in therapy twenty years from now.

Also, I have since learned a lot of dark truths about the horrors of these dolphin programs, how the dolphins were taken from their mothers too young and it

---

* Dated technological and cultural references such as this one to YouTube.com are necessary to connect with contemporary readers, and I apologize to those reading me hundreds or, dare I say, thousands of years after publication.

made them turn violent and start raping other sea creatures. See, even dolphins have misplaced aggression. Or was that the elephants with the rhinoceroses? Anyway, sad stuff, real upsetting. But at least the animals are expressing their emotions. And I'm trying to do the same, but only because it's my time to do so.

For all of you, the little pre-depressos out there, you've got to wait until it's your time. You can't skip the repression phase. You need to reach your depression phase in order to begin healing through your full-on adult tantrum phase, so *wait your turn*. It's no fun to be a big baby as an adult when you were already a big baby as an actual baby. When in doubt, make this your mantra: "Repress, repress, repress."

....

CHAPTER FIVE

HELL IS OTHER KIDS:
DEVELOP A SOCIAL ANXIETY ON THE PLAYGROUND THAT WILL COME IN HANDY AS AN ADULT

This is important: *Don't forget to water the anxiety plant.*

Even as a child. Being social, interacting with other kids, the pressure may not be the same as when you're an adult trying to navigate some ridiculous cocktail party. But have you been to a playground lately? It's survival of the fittest out there.

Social anxiety and depression intertwine in unexpected ways, and if you want to experience a complete depression, you'll have to start fueling it as early as possible with states of heightened anxiety.

Some folks see anxiety as the opposite of depression. But I find all structures of duality fall away in the unified plane that is depression. Isn't that convenient? Truly, there's plenty of room inside your weeping, curled-up shell of a self for agitated thoughts and stomach-churning nerves. In fact, anxiety can be an excellent gateway emotion to depression.

When I was eight, I used to dread Saturday soccer practice and the Sunday games with such ferocity that on the car trip to the field, I would stare out the window, look at some weeds growing in the soil on the highway divider, and pray to switch places with the forlorn, dust-covered dandelion. If only the flower could go play the soccer game for me, and I could stay there, swaying in the soft breeze when traffic was light and occasionally getting blown exuberantly horizontal when a truck barreled past.

Fantasies of switching souls with inanimate objects still come upon me when I'm expected to do something like attend a dinner. Most often the object I identify with is some sort of amorphous lump, which makes sense since I'm lying around so much. But I would suggest you not limit yourself.

Now, that doesn't mean you should go crazy: I would never advise you to go from thinking you're a lump to thinking you're a real swell dude. But there is a wide range of nonhuman objects out there for you to imagine yourself as.

. . . .

TOP SIX WAYS TO SEE YOURSELF, OTHER THAN AS A USELESS LUMP

1. A deck of cards, shuffled and set aside, full of possibility
2. A turtle
3. A tiny turtle riding on the back of a large

turtle—a turtle so large, in fact, that you don't even realize you're moving

4. Pure nature. Not civilized human. Not part of society or culture. Just raw nature itself. Like a tree or a star or a sea creature. Nothing is expected of you from the universe. (You're much closer to the truth of existence when you curl up and do nothing but breathe. You're much more urchin than schmuck.)

5. A discarded doll. An old dusty porcelain Suzy who sits awkwardly propped or lies face down, basically begging for demonic possession by a passing hellion. Pretend you're one of those dolls and you haven't been touched in thirty-five years. You must affix your gaze and not blink. It's creepy and kind of fun.

6. A puddle. You know that thing about how your body is 80 percent water? It could be interesting for a few minutes to really get that through your head and then lie there and feel yourself as what you really are: a puddle.

· ·

You only get better at these soul-switching fantasies as you become an older, more experienced depressive. And once you're an adult, you have what they call "agency," which means you can unravel your own life at any moment and neglect on a whim your obligations and responsibilities to others. You can actually set up life on a highway divider, among the weeds, and get away with it, at least until the cops show up.

The freedom to mess up your own life if you damn well please is something all you depressed kids can look forward to. When you grow up, there are no annoying school systems, guidance counselors, and child social services to stop you from doing what you want to do, like eating ice cream at three a.m., but more important, from *not* doing what you don't want to do . . . dropping out of school, quitting ballet, renouncing your Girl Scout vows.

In fact, to this day the only thing that sometimes helps me get through some pizza dinner (where no one *ever* orders enough and I lack the courage to protest) is to remind myself, *At least it's not soccer practice.*

Ugh, the soccer. Why did I do it if I hated it so much? When I was a kid, Dad always emphasized the importance of seeing through to the end the activities I had committed to. And I think that's a reasonable expectation. But then for some insane reason, after sticking it out until the season was over, I would also invariably—out of some early masochistic impulse, no doubt—sign up again for the next year!

Once I got to high school, it was a little better. Field hockey, my high school sport, was a daily activity, which afforded me less time to develop anxiety between practices. But as a kid, I had all week to build up my dread of the upcoming soccer game.

I don't know why I continued playing sports at all. I was clearly meant for the arts. I wish more of you kids knew that sports are not as essential as childhood propaganda suggests. Not long ago, I saw a little girl crying at a swim meet, and it took everything in me not to go up to her and whisper, "Have you considered a life in the theater?"

I also considered quitting field hockey after every season, but then when summer would draw to a close, I'd find myself showing up for six a.m. preseason training. Maybe I was in it for the kilts. I couldn't resist the lure of a new, hopefully shorter one. Attracting the attention of boy crushes by revealing my toned hamstrings was a real priority, and our kilts were orange, so they served as road flares for our bodies.

Preseason was two weeks of twice-a-day conditioning and practice sessions, sometimes followed up by a weeklong stint at a field hockey camp. There are benefits to being in forced labor settings. The hellish total immersion gave me no caloric energy to burn on dread, and so I'd get into the rhythm out of necessity.

This is what people talk about when they tell you to "throw yourself into an activity." The idea is to do something with such frequency or fervor that you never have time to contemplate how miserable it makes you. Even today, when I hear folks talk about throwing themselves into activities, it makes me think of lemmings going off a cliff. I look at my friends who don't suffer depression and compare their healthy habits to my own dysfunction (a great practice in and of itself) and I think, who *are* these people?

These are the types who will see an unheated pool, recklessly dive in, and then laughingly tell you: "It's only cold for a second, then it's really warm." My friend Laura does this all the time. Treading water after a dive, she smoothes her soaked hair away from her face, eyes shining, and calls for you to "trust her."

Here's how I face the pool . . . and life. I dip in a toe and then retreat, eventually circling back to plant myself on the first step of the submerged staircase. Clinging to the warm metal banister, I ease down a step at a time, trying to skip that horrible moment when the water reaches the waist and it feels as if you've been cut in half. Meanwhile, I'm getting splashed by all the psychopaths who followed Laura's advice and cannonballed in.

Sometimes, I buy in to the Nike way and I just do it. I even cannonball, but gently. I would never try to splash an onlooker. The thing is, I know in my heart it's not my style. Briefly, once in the water, I'll wonder if this is how I'll be from here on out. I mean, it does get you in the water faster. But at the same time, it's disorienting—you hardly even recognize yourself. Who is this person enjoying the cool submersion?

If you are looking to foster anxiety and social dread on a more regular basis in your life, you must follow my lead and take the proverbial pool stairs over the cannonball at all costs. When you "throw yourself" into friendships, activities, basically anything other than your depression, you risk obscuring your true mood. But only for so long.

Even if you recognize yourself as a cannonballer for life . . . the great thing about depression is that it can still find its way back to you. It's incredibly adaptable. It can figure out how to make even a cannonball joyless. Take comfort in that.

....

CHAPTER SIX

NIGHTLIGHT CHATS WITH A HALF-JEWISH GOD: THE DEPRESSIVE-IN-TRAINING'S GUIDE TO FAITH

I once read (overheard in line at the pharmacy) that not being baptized as a baby can lead to depressions later in life. According to whatever trustworthy source it was, the soul can feel ungrounded, like it's suddenly at the gym, absentmindedly stroking the kettlebells, knowing it never swiped its membership at the front desk. So if any of you youngsters are able to avoid or botch a baptism, hey, it might help get your soul on board with the depression.

I was not baptized, nor did I enter into any religious school (Hebrew or Sunday), probably because my parents just wanted to keep us out of the muck of religion. Religion had been the source of a lot of drama for my parents, when my mom, daughter of a conservative rabbi, married my father, a non-Jew. We celebrated "all the holidays," as I would explain to both my Christian and Jewish friends.

As for ideas about God, my mom said something about it being a helpful idea to those who believed. My dad said that God was everywhere—and, yes, that included my ear—and that God, along with Mom and Dad, had "made" me. Ew, like a threesome with a polyamorous zealot.

As for my own attempts to connect with God, well, He betrayed me the one time I asked Him for something that seemed completely reasonable. I was going through a fear-of-death stage. I was about eight at the time. Lying in bed, staring at my Glowworm night-light and considering Shelley Long's choking death in *Hello Again,* I began to panic.

I gripped the bars of my headboard like a prisoner of Life and loudly (in my head) asked Him to strike me down right then and there. The anxiety of not knowing when in my life death would come for me was too much to handle. I'd rather just die right then than live a long, full life of waiting and wondering.

Of course, God flatly refused. Or He didn't hear me or didn't exist. Whatever the reason, moments later I was decidedly still there, in my bed, forced to turn on the light and read a Baby-Sitter's Club book to soothe my mind.

In retrospect, I am relieved He didn't kill me, but I would have appreciated a more personalized no, a visitation by a fairy godhorse or some other animal guide. I wasn't interested in a godmother or godfather. Who wants to form friendships with strange adults?

This hatred of anticipation would later emerge as a defining trait and one of my biggest depression themes. But as a child, there were already hints. I would listen to cassette tapes in bed at night before I fell asleep and be irrationally bothered by the silence at the end of each side of the tape. The last song on a side would end, and then there'd be fifteen to thirty seconds before the tape reached its true end and the button clicked from PLAY to STOP.

Well, I hated waiting for that loud click. I would struggle with whether to hop up, race over to the boom box, and press STOP myself or just wait for it, bracing myself in my bed. The worst thing that could possibly happen would be to get up to go press STOP and have it click while I was in motion. Surely I'd scream.

The same kind of terror would strike when I was waiting for a pizza to cook in the microwave. I'd pop in my Celeste Pizza for One and go to the bathroom while it cooked. Then suddenly I'd be overcome with anxiety over not knowing how much time had passed or when the beeps were coming. I'd race to the kitchen to press CANCEL before it ended on its own.

And no, I did not enjoy the game Operation. There was no joy in the surprise of that infirmed fool's buzzer.

Eventually, these childhood anxieties blossomed into one of my favorite depression-inducing behaviors, which all pre-depressos will want to have in their arsenal. In the common tongue, it's called self-sabotage, but that makes it sound like such a bummer. It's really the depressive's chief form of recreation.

It's similar to the cannonball jump into the water, where you throw yourself right into the activity you fear. But instead, you throw yourself into the *failure* you fear, in order to get over it. Then you feel at peace, knowing the outcome, no matter how bad.

When I had asked God to put me out of my misery as a child, that was a perfect, all-encompassing, triple Axel example of self-sabotage. But alas, He was unwilling, so I was forced to pick up the mantle and begin my lifelong practice of day-to-day sabotage.

The "kill me now" chat is the only conversation I recall having with God as a child. Not a ton of prayer. At night, my dad would tuck me in by speedily spitting out the Lord's Prayer, faster than the legal disclaimers at the end of an automobile ad. But he wanted me to know it. As a child, he had been shamed when asked to recite it at a friend's house and didn't know it, and he didn't want that to happen to me. I listened and lightly contemplated the words, always thinking the words were "Thy kingdom come, *I* will be done," meaning "when I die, I'll head to your place."

My mom's main spiritual offering to me seemed to be Jewish fear. I always connected my mom's anxieties with her having been raised by Conservative Jews. Every Jewish family member I know seems to carry with them an unspoken belief that fear can save you. Worrying about a disease lets God know that if He gives it to you, you won't be surprised, so He might as well just skip the effort. A watched cell never metastasizes.

That whole AA "Let Go and Let God" slogan is something I've never heard out of the mouth of an old-school Jew. Even carried on the breath of whitefish salad and cloaked in the most pronounced New York Jewish accent, "Let Go and Let God" doesn't sound authentic.

The Jews seem to hold a belief that fear is a gift, probably from God, and yet they can't quite relax and trust in their fear. I've decided it's due to some twist on the Achilles myth. God dipped the Jews in a substance called fear to protect them. God probably dipped the males by the foreskin, and this is why circumcision is so important. It chops off the one little body part that isn't coated in protective fear.

Maybe the girls are dipped by their noses, which God made more prominent so He could have a good grip. Then He instilled in other parts of the world a standard of beauty that never quite accepted the aesthetic. He knew that many of His creations of the female Jewish variety who ended up far from home would remove the handle through rhinoplasty and therefore be safer.

For both the men and women of the Tribe, God ensured that they would suffer no hole in their armor of fear. All-encompassing fear is a great environment to activate a young OCD'er to ensure she is deeply aware of the very thin line that stands between her merely picking up a knife or actually stabbing herself.

Oh, look at me mythologizing! Religion is fun, as long as I'm the one making it up, which just might be the key for the young depresso: avoid religion or start your own. It can be very profitable.

As a kid I was jealous of the Catholics, who I imagined as always praying. My town didn't have a lot of Catholics, so I mostly knew their ways from television. I was always drawn to the idea of running off to Confession, shutting myself in the booth, removing my cloak, kneeling solemnly, and saying, "Bless me, Father, for I have sinned." Must be something about the kneeling. I've never had the opportunity to fall to my knees in spiritual awe like in "Oh, Holy Night." I've tried to force it when listening to a particularly moving guided meditation, but it's awkward to both fake a collapse and enjoy it.

Spiritual awe may be something you can't force, but depression-filled anguish is something I've never had to force, and that's an equally appropriate time to fall to one's knees.

But if only I had been raised Catholic, not only would I be falling to my knees, I'd be doing *all* of the cool shit: mumbling "Thy will be done" and kissing my cross necklace. Not sure why, but imagining myself Catholic makes me feel like a character in a dramatic film.

Maybe religion just has an over-the-top, all-or-nothing quality about it that is attractive to depressives like me who are drawn to extremes. In religion they're always talking about mercy. That's an exciting word to a depressive. It's so massive. There aren't enough opportunities in modern American life to beg for mercy.

Later in the book we will talk about how adult depression can be a great opportunity for dipping your toe into whatever the hell religious or spiritual practice you feel like. You're at your lowest, you're humbled and desperate. What better time to become attached to false idols and yoga teachers with pert butts that fill out sheer-linen movement pants.

Best of all, you'll be free to pick and choose whatever rituals sound fun, and even make stuff up like me.

But for now, work with whatever you've got. Maybe you were raised, as I was, without much religious ritual (I never had a bat mitzvah, for example, but I grew up in Westchester, so I've heard my fair share of butchered *haftarah* readings by warbly adolescents). Maybe you didn't have the same awesome direct access to religious guilt, et cetera, as your more devout ancestors. I, for one, can only dream of having something to support my fears and neuroses like my grandfather did with his overidentification with the prophet Job and other biblical shit that I'm barely familiar with.

That's why, even if you don't personally have a comforting ideological framework as a kid to help foster your future depression, chances are your parents grew up with religion, and with a bit of effort, you can tap in to all of *their* faith-based anxieties and pathologies.

Whatever your childhood circumstances may be—if you attend a church or a mosque or are a member of one of those new atheist churches—religion is a great way to add a whole new range of disturbing symptoms and behaviors to your future depressive repertoire.

....

CHAPTER SEVEN

BIRTHDAY WISHES:
THAT MY TENTH B-DAY PASS
BY UNMENTIONED

When I was about fourteen, my mom said, "You have your whole life ahead of you. You can be anything you want to be."

I slurred through my braces: "Not a gymnast. Too late—they start early."

At seventeen, I was upset that the tune "Sixteen Candles" no longer applied to me. Even at the age of three, I was mourning having missed the chance to be the new face of Gerber. But I was just being realistic. Windows are closing all the time. Even in the brief moment you are pausing to consider this, more are closing.

Conventional wisdom is that birthdays only start becoming an issue when you get older; when you're young, you want to be a big boy or big girl, the sooner the better. But I say no, if you want to help develop your depression early, you have to use even your childhood birthdays to flagellate yourself over the opportunities you've already missed.

One way I managed to do this as a kid was to deliberately put myself in situations in which I felt behind, even very early in life. I surrounded myself with professional children, for example, at acting camp. These little fuckers were the real cream of the crop, getting picked up by car services to go audition for commercials while the rest of us marched to the meal hall. No matter how hard I worked, I knew I would never be as good as them. It was already too late.

This fundamental truth of human existence—it's already too late—always seemed to pop up for me around birthdays, particularly when it came to presents. My parents would ask what I wanted as a gift. If they said, "Let's get you a guitar," I'd contemplate it and then shake my head. I knew I wasn't two anymore, and there were other kids who started playing guitar at the age of two. It was already too late for me—I'd never be as good as them. I'd prefer a gigantic Hershey's Kiss, please.

In the years since, I've changed my thinking on this a bit. Don't get me wrong: I haven't become all "seize the day" on you. I am still consumed most days by overwhelming, disgusting regret. I still think the old saying "It's never too late" is bullshit. The real truth is both worse and more freeing—not that it's never too late, but that it's *always* too late, so you might as well go ahead and take up the guitar or whatever the hell you want to do.

Think of it this way: Why be jealous of the kid who started playing guitar at age two? He ain't got that many years on you in the grand scheme of things. Consider that once you've both been dead for even a little over two hundred years, the small amount of time that either of you got to play the guitar is already dwarfed by your time in the grave. If he got in forty years of guitar, and you got in only twenty, fractionally he's barely got any time on you. Even better, as time marches on, that ratio gets smaller.

So, yeah, right now maybe he seems like the big winner with his fingers flying across those strings while you sit there struggling to make a C chord, but don't worry—you'll both be rotting soon.

When you consider the eternity of death, you realize it's really too late to do anything at all, even live. Time is running out. Every single strum of a guitar is, in a grand sense, actually violin music on the *Titanic*.

. . . .

TOP NINE BIRTHDAY PRESENTS FOR THE CHILD DEPRESSIVE-IN-TRAINING

1. Jack-in-the-box, classic clown face. Offers an early opportunity to explore the anxiety of anticipation. As all depressives worth their salt understand, knowing something will happen but not knowing *when* can fill one with a far greater dread than is appropriate.

2. Ouija board. Some say this can legitimately invite in demons to suck out your life force.

3. Doll that records and repeats what you say, thus mirroring the internal critic but in a more tangible form for the still-developing ego.

4. "Freud for Kids." A guide to zipping through the fecal phase and latency period at double speed so you can get started with sexual individuation early and be labeled one of the "fast kids" in your class.

5. Magic Eye poster with no embedded image. Will frustrate and confuse but ultimately teaches an important lesson: even if there is meaning to life, you'll never have the ability to access it.

6. Goldfish stuffed animal. Won't die, and unlike a fish, you can hug it.

7. White noise machine. For privacy when playing. No need to be judged.

8. Cello. Its somber, haunting tones might be the only way for the youngster to accurately express himself in later years.

9. Zip line. Another quality lesson. Have fun but keep your feet out. Learn the art of flying free with exuberance while always remembering to be afraid of slamming into the tree.

. . . .

Well, I'm glad we've cleared that one up. The notion of "time passing you by" is essentially untrue, even in your later life as a depressed adult lying on the floor like a pile of dirty laundry. The difference between you and your more accomplished childhood friends—at the age of three, eight, or twelve—is minor in the grand scheme of things.

Or to put it another way, no matter how many years you think you've "lost," whether to being a worthless sloth of a child or a proper adult depressive, there are folks who are losing those same numbers of years as a prisoner of war or lying in a coma. Take comfort in the fact that even if you're doing absolutely nothing with your life, you're probably getting more done than them.

Whenever I want to remind myself that life is long enough to offset any dark period, I think of my parents' neighbor in the sunny burbs, a Holocaust survivor who once leapt from an Auschwitz-bound train and lived in a cemetery, where he dug bones and ate the marrow. The story doesn't end there. The Nazis caught him in the graveyard, but he escaped a second time, and then again once more. I may have the details wrong, but I can tell you he made it out eventually—and has since won the lottery and purchased a red sports car.*

When I was living at my folks' house, utterly smothered in my depressed haze, I'd often see this man walking the neighborhood, and we'd smile at each other. We were both at home during the day, and there was something steadying about the slow suburban sun rolling

_____

* I know it doesn't seem possible, but this story is true.

over the two of us, morning upon morning, after what we had been through in our lives.

Yes, you heard me, I just compared my cozy coalescence at my parents' house to his flight from genocide. But really, what I mean to suggest is that my neighbor seemed to be enjoying himself in a rather traditional way. His long Holocaust journey didn't even prevent him later in life from taking joy in something as conventionally material and meaningless as a fancy automobile. If he could go from eating human bone marrow to caring about the color of a sports car, then maybe one day my moody stint could feel remote.

Passing Mr. Z in the cul-de-sac—he, a spritely, cheerful, elderly survivor, and I, a shuffling, moody, but technically able-bodied young woman—brought up some questions. First, it made me ashamed. He suffered some of the worst horrors imaginable and seemed to be doing great. I have not suffered, and I can barely stand up.

But then I'd remind myself, depression is a disorder, feel cheered up, and quickly move on to my next point of quandary. Specifically, how would I have fared in the Holocaust? Can you imagine if you were already clinically depressed in your regular life and *then* were put in a death camp? Your bunkmates would have no patience for hearing about your special melancholy. They'd say, "You sure it's not the whole death camp thing? None of us is exactly psyched to be in here." No one would believe you. It would be awkward. Real insult to injury.

And worse, what if all the physical labor at the camp

gave you some mood reprieve, strictly clinically speaking? Would you try to hide it? It's not like you would advertise, "I gotta be honest, guys, I haven't felt this good in a long, long time!" As any depressed person has heard over and over again, the endorphins released through exercise can serve as an antidepressant. But would that still apply if you'd been prodded into the exercise with a rifle in your back? I'm betting it would.

According to my mom, my grandfather Zaidie, serving as a chaplain in World War II, taking part in the liberation of the concentration camps, really perked up during the war. Depressives might just be built for abject horror, and in the absence of hideousness, we suffer. In that way, what pleasure could a nice guitar habit even bring?

....

CHAPTER EIGHT

SCHOOL:
A HIDEOUS MICROCOSM OF
THE WORLD

The worst thing about school is that you have to go. I don't even consider prison to be an *analogy* for school; it is simply its most natural *definition,* and this statement comes from someone who "loves to learn." If school had been optional—if I had been given the choice to go to Roaring Brook Elementary *or* work on my parents' farm (assuming they had a farm)—I would have loved school and chosen to go there. After all, a dark, cool library in the summer can be very pleasant.

But knowing one *must* go, that school is an inevitability as implacable as death, makes it a chilling proposition. For a sensitive youngster, it's a real shock to the senses, almost a second birth, in which you're split from the relative womb of your home, and your family, into a colder, larger context that smells weird.

Worst of all, there's the structure—advancing through the grades, taking quizzes, getting report cards, having to interact with other children through hunger-terror games like Steal the Bacon. Suddenly, you've been dropped from the natural, fluid world of home onto a kind of grid where you can assess your worth from a thousand directions, on a number of scales.

To top it off, there's nowhere to hide. Everything plays out in front of everyone else. The crushing discomfort is profound, but you don't yet have the language to find common ground over suffering. Hey, other kids! Isn't first grade deeply alienating? You know the teachers really should have initiated more group dialogue about how terrifying school is.

It sounds silly, but if we had spoken to one another that way, acknowledging we were in prison, we probably could have gotten more comfortable with the idea and celebrated the ways our prison was preferable to Sing Sing.

The one benefit of the hell of early schooling is that it familiarizes you with the feeling of being powerless and unequipped, with nowhere to hide—which is very similar to being an adult depressive with, say, a job. The skills you are forced to develop to survive in school might be useful in helping keep you afloat later in life. That is *if*, at any point, keeping afloat is in fact your goal. You never know.

I personally took great comfort in engaging in activities in the public setting of school that only I was aware of. I liked to create private spaces in plain sight.

For example, you know the little space underneath your desk at school, where you keep your notebooks, et cetera? I would perform elaborate plays in that little cubby, Shakespearian tragedies with my thumbs as the starring puppets, the erasers and pencils as members of the chorus.

I'd delight in the fact that only I knew what was going on. Okay, maybe those intricate plays were in fact one-acts that sometimes only lasted a few seconds. But even knowing there was a theater, even an off-season dark theater, inside my desk gave me a feeling of inner warmth.

And if I was away from my desk, I could set up the traveling theater in my mouth, behind my teeth, with my tongue playing all the parts. Even making motions with my tongue inside my closed mouth was a secret little act that I treasured.

If something was stressing me out, I'd write in tiny letters inside my notebook, on the next notebook page, to be discovered the following day, the letters *HDIFN*, which stood for "How Do I Feel Now?" Then I'd discover that the thing bothering me one day had usually worked itself out by the following day.

These self-soothing little behaviors did help me survive the day, but once I got comfortable enough to tolerate being there, I started to look around at other kids and yearn for more. Surviving wasn't enough. I wanted to self-actualize. I believed I could, hoping that I wasn't so much inherently flawed as not yet seen for who I was.

School is, if nothing else, a place where the sensitive go to be misunderstood.

In first grade, I tried to win the affection of my teacher and peers by bringing in a humor piece I'd crafted. It was an utterly on-point satire of flowery writing I'd worked very hard on. I had spent many weekend hours on my dad's Apple making it the best it could be, laughing as I wrote.

The teacher was impressed and insisted on reading it to the whole class. But to my dismay, he missed the whole point. Instead of hailing me a young Voltaire, he presented it to my classmates as an example of great vivid writing. I was mortified as he read aloud, without a hint of irony, my descriptions of lily pads floating on the lake like clouds.

I knew I had to begin the uncomfortable work of reforming myself to become someone I could face in the bus window's reflection each morning. My parents' general message of "be yourself, try your hardest," was not going to cut it. So I took the next natural step for a second grader: I delved into the world of self-help literature.

Yes, self-help books, or Success Literature, have been part of my world almost as long as I can remember. Even at the age of seven, before I knew such a genre existed, I longed for it. I scoured the shelves of the Roaring Brook Elementary School library for a title that would provide the answers I was searching for.

No luck. There was nothing, no nonfiction guide to

taking step-by-step actions toward greatness, unless you count a book about how to build an authentic teepee. If you wanted to explore the great questions of one's own existence, you had to find them indirectly, buried inside narratives like *Tuck Everlasting*.

Then, finally, one day I came across a book that seemed to be just what I was looking for. The spine read, *How to Be a Perfect Person in Just Three Days*. I wanted to be perfect; perfection didn't sound bad at all. And here was a book that would tell me how to do it. But it turned out to be the fictional story of a boy's misguided attempt. So fucking typical. I was annoyed, but I took it home anyway.

Buried inside, in a very meta way, the book did contain some answers. It actually told the story of a boy checking out the very same book from his library, so at least the book within the book was a legitimate guide. I hoped there would be direct quotes.

It was something, but it wasn't what I was looking for. Where was *my* legitimate guide? If a children's library is going to stock a book that responds creatively and self-consciously to the idea of self-help books, shouldn't it also include a few books in the original genre? How are you going to stock a humorous retelling of *Hamlet* but not *Hamlet*?

Nonetheless, I gave *Perfect* a shot. I tried to get what I was looking for out of it. I already knew that the moral was the opposite of what I wanted. Of course, the lesson was going to be that you don't need to be perfect. But I wanted to be perfect. So I paid special attention to the misguided protagonist's early follies, before he learned his lesson. This was tricky work. It was like trying to learn how to avoid having sex with your mother by reading only the first part of *Oedipus Rex*.

The universe clearly heard my intentions, however, because soon afterward I came across the answer to my prayers, the mother lode of self-help: Anthony (Tony) Robbins's Personal Power series. My dad's friend lent my family all forty-odd cassette tapes. My dad was starting his own business, and his friend thought Tony could help. Dad listened in the car, and I rode around even more rapt.

That was the beginning of a lifelong love affair with Tony Robbins. I have a profound affection for this man that no one can take away. Even if Tony himself assaulted me, I would stand by his work. And hearing him on the cassettes was so much better than just reading the words. I was moved by the way his voice would grow hoarse at the most emotional moments, and sometimes even full-on crack. He must have been so passionate about sharing his "tools of mastery" that he didn't have a chance to drink any water in the studio.

That's just how selfless Tony is. This hulking man was so wrapped up in helping you that he'd forget to hydrate his instrument and would be reduced to practically squeaking, "If you can conceive it, you can achieve it."

Listening to Tony as a young girl was a surreal experience. A lot of the anecdotes were not exactly relatable at that age, like his stories about people who wanted to quit smoking. But it made me feel good to be so ahead of the curve. I would imagine the smokers who came to Tony for help and feel sorry for those poor adult bastards who were only coming around to Tony's guidance now. Not me, I was learning Tony's skills early, so I could practice them in the elementary school arena, hone them in middle school, and unleash the Giant Within in time to straight-up dominate high school.

I just knew that Tony was the answer to my problems. People like to shit on this guy and on self-help in general. Basically, there are two kinds of people: those who read self-help and those who think self-help is for losers. Some would say those two groups are made up of, respectively, losers and nonlosers. I agree, except I think the ones who think self-helpies are losers are the *real* losers, my friends. I high-five myself, and miss.

I did successfully apply Tony's principles over the middle school years and was quite a star in the eighth grade. Not so much publicly, but I was having private victories left and right. And as Stephen Covey, author of the classic *7 Habits of Highly Effective People* says, "private victories precede public victories."

By then I was supplementing with a variety of texts in the genre. I had done a lot of fine work, having knocked the legs out from under a number of my limiting beliefs and begun to live from new, neurolinguistically programmed power statements.

I jogged every day, noted in my journal all the ways I wanted to be a better person, and always performed the required personal inventory and goal assessment from the recommended altitudes of perspective at each quarter year.

My biggest achievement, however, was this: I forced my way into Advanced Math.

Even though I hadn't tested high enough to get into Advanced Math, I insisted I be admitted. Other people would not define my reality, nor would I let the test terror that no doubt had plagued me on that unfateful day at the end of the previous year compromise my education. In Tony's wise words: "The past does not equal the future."

On the first day of school, even though my schedule clearly said Math 8 not Math 8A, I marched into the principal's office and demanded to be put in the advanced class. They were flustered and so just waved me off and told me to go to the class, the advanced one.

I walked out of the office with a determined little grin on my face. But it would not last. When I opened the door to the math room, not only was I ten minutes late, but the teacher noticed immediately I wasn't on the roster and said in front of the whole class: "Oh, you must be one of those kids whose parents made a big stink over their little baby not being put in Smart Math. Not *my* kid. No, *my* kid's a genius."

I wanted to shout out: *No, it was me, it wasn't them. I was the one to make a stink.* I resented the fact that he assumed my parents were behind this, when in fact it had been rooted in my own admirable drive to succeed.

Instead, all I said to the crabby hardass teacher, as my stomach twisted in knots like Ursula's eels, was "No, I'm *meant* to be here." I held back hot tears for the duration of the class, then speed-walked to the "8th Grade Bathroom" and hiccup-sobbed, diaphragm bucking.

The ending of this story is that I got a 98 on the Regents Exam that year.

You heard me.

The story and its heroic conclusion are exemplary of my frame of mind at the time and in the years that followed. I was so determined to prove people wrong—and to prove to myself that I could conquer the demon of my encroaching depression through the magic sword of Tony—that I became a kind of shoulder-padded, workaholic type who'd forgotten her sensual self and alienated husband and family, all to "make partner" . . . long before I'd been kissed. I needed to Rudy my way into that class not because I saw a future for myself in math, but because I could not abide the idea of not being the self-help warrior I saw myself as.

Depression makes you blow things way out of proportion, and in my case it made me inappropriately attached in high school to ideas like "perfect SAT scores equal moral superiority." I simply refused to allow for the possibility that all the book wisdom I had acquired might not be my salvation, that I might not be like the people in Tony's testimonials who became the selves they wanted to be through the sheer force of their determination.

In one of Tony's stories, he talks about a guy who had a motorcycle accident, became paralyzed, lost his hands, got his toes sewn onto his palms to serve as fingers, and then the cherry on top . . . his wife left him. But the story has a happy ending. The guy not only survived but thrived in a variety of ways that seem designed to appeal to Tony's students (that is, making a lot of money and marrying an even more beautiful woman, with bigger tits than the first).

Tits aside, the story moved me. If this guy could win, surely I could succeed at whatever I put my mind to accomplishing. I started writing mission statements, from which I drew up weekly and then daily goals (for example, get a six-pack like TLC, specifically T-Boz's).

I also began going on longer runs. I recall a sports bra I had at the time, black with a white Nike swoosh. I thought it was the most beautiful thing. Now keep in mind I've always shied away from garments with a minimizing bosom, as they make my potbellied stomach stand out. But this sports bra was so chic I didn't care! I would strip down to the bra and shorts and jog through the neighborhood with sweaty abandon.

I'd listen to nostalgic tunes like "Brown Eyed Girl" and "Son of a Preacher Man"; new instant classics like Destiny's Child's "Survivor"; any of the masterpieces off the Jock Jams compilations; and the occasional Personal Power audio. The music would lift me like a slow-moving wave, as I'd ponder my wide-open future. I was only a teenager, but I was already like an emotional ninja, ready to slice my way out of the weeds of any so-called problem and into whatever new garden of life awaited me.

When I'd hear the gravel drag of a car about to pass me, I'd veer off and give it room, jogging in place, as it drove by. I couldn't really see the faces in the car, but I felt sorry for them, even projected on them a sort of death. These people in their cars were living out the dullness of their adulthood, no doubt choking under a life that grew out of limiting beliefs. *Poor bastards.*

Then I'd put my headphones back on and continue running, letting a little smile out. I was on my way. *Unstoppable.*

That's how I recall my mindset in the high school years, long before the full-on adult depression would drag me down to the depths. Yes, I had already seen the darkness, I knew life was scary, and I knew I had to be careful. But I was confident in my self-awareness. I thought I had learned enough to cope. I wasn't going to let anything stop me from having whatever success I imagined for myself.

It's not that I was in denial about my sensitive, neurotic self; I'd been that way since I was a baby. But I knew that when troubles sprang up, I could sit down with a journal, my exercises, and parse it out with a variety of self-help texts to refer to.

Nothing—math classes, delayed breast development, unexpected crushes on school admins—was beyond the scope of these paradigms (which I mispronounced *para-diggums* for far too long). I had learned from Tony that everything was a matter of how you choose to look at it. Life was up to you.

Best of all, I no longer identified as just a highly sensitive little freak constantly adrift in a cold world. Every problem that popped up, I could work out, in my success journal, with my favorite gurus by my side. I knew that as a man thinketh, so he reapeth. I pitied and attempted to educate my friends who let their lives be dictated by circumstances, sometimes forcing them to listen to a Tony tape as we did our homework on my bedroom floor.

I was really something, and I'm a bit nostalgic for that girl. She really had it figured out. Personal responsibility was her highest value.

But as you know, she had not been reading the Book of Proverbs. Pride, in her mind, did not goeth before the fall. It was merely the appropriate emotional confidence of someone who had learned how to attack life, transcend troubles. Someone who could always find a way to kick ass and take names.

If you can achieve self-actualization as a tween or teen, before depression hits, it will really make for a more dramatic fall later on. A little misanthropic mope who trips into depression is easy to dismiss as merely moody. They're more likely to slip naturally into depression without a sound.

But if you can become a dynamo by eighth grade,

a little blowhard mini-guru, maybe with your own YouTube channel, your descent into depression will be uglier, or more beautiful, depending on how you look at it. Perhaps you will rage, rage against the dying of the light, which can make for an interesting few years.

At least that's how I did it. And advice is usually just that: do what I did so I feel less alone.

. . . .

A FEW GOOD BOOKS
FOR THE DEPRESSED

1. *Cognitive Therapy and the Emotional Disorders,* by Aaron T. Beck. Shows you exactly the kind of cognitive errors that you and other depressos tend to make.

2. *Wherever You Go, There You Are,* by Jon Kabat-Zinn. Only problem with this book is that the title sounds idiotic to outsiders.

3. *The Van Gogh Blues,* by Eric Maisel. Basic idea is artists are people who dismantle idea systems, but this often also includes their own reasons for living—that is, "nothing means anything" leads to "fuck taxes, off I go to bed."

4. *Undoing Depression,* by Richard O'Connor. I love this book, but all I remember about it is that when the author was depressed, he took taxis everywhere, and so did I. Descending stairs to a subway system is too much. Sometimes I'll

shuffle along three miles to a destination just to avoid that underworld.

5. *Against Depression,* by Peter D. Kramer. A great book to give to assholes (and there are many) who deny that clinical depression is a real pathology affecting your brain.

. . . .

PART TWO

HOW TO CULTIVATE YOUR DEPRESSION AS A YOUNG ADULT

If your childhood is all about planting the seeds of your future depression, then the high school and college years are about finally starting to experience its bloom—and then trying desperately, and ultimately unsuccessfully, to outrun it. But for now, take comfort in the fact that the exquisitely depressed person that's been trapped inside you all this time is finally coming out.

In my case, depression came on like a spiteful attempt by the gods (I become more pagan by the hour) to disabuse me of the belief that I was master of my destiny. It was a real crap thing to do. After all, I'd worked hard to topple my childhood neuroses. And now, instead of basking in greatness, I was about to be struck down. Because I was a half Jew, some of that protective fear had been diluted, and now I was suffering the consequences.

Young adulthood is a shit show in general, during which you're expected to both grow and learn while also preparing for a future. No! The best you can try to do is stay afloat in that torrential shit. I'm using a buoy-type metaphor here, but chances are you're not in the water so much as flat on the floor, crying into your hands. Particularly if you went into young adulthood with a bold swagger, ready to tackle any problems with the skills you'd achieved as a master human by eighth grade.

If knowledge is power, I was a She-Ra. When I started to experience heavy depression symptoms, I was truly confused and knew I just must not be thinking right. You didn't have to tell me about thinking positive; I was a scholar of *success*.

Whenever concerned adults tried to offer advice, I wanted to smack them over the head with my self-help books. I was already way beyond them. I was using Robbins's anchoring techniques to put myself in a state of passion. I was working the 7 Habits, "seeking to understand, not to be understood." I was doing it all.

But there I was on the floor, face on the cat, unable to handle the decision of whether or not to take a shower. I'd be reviewing all the things I was grateful for and still feeling unable to stand. Had one of the Tony tapes slipped between the car seat and the center console? Something was very wrong. Even though nothing was wrong.

The problem, as I learned through my teens and into my early twenties, was that all the knowledge in the world can't protect you from depression. It is a worthy foe, if you can identify it at all. And once you do, you'll probably attempt to outrun it. It's natural. You flee before you fight. That's even a principle in Krav Maga.

But running makes you tired, and when you're tired you make mistakes, you do embarrassing shit, you screw up. But at the time, so does everyone else, so in the end it's fine. Young adulthood is like a crowded dance class where everybody's busy watching herself fuck up the body roll.

....

CHAPTER NINE

YOUR FIRST THERAPIST:
CONVINCE HER THAT SHE FIXED YOU AT THE END OF EVERY SESSION, THEN GO HOME FOR MORE SUFFERING

High school is also the time that burgeoning depressives are often introduced to their first counselors and therapists. If this is you, it feels good, doesn't it? You've come a long way. You're no longer just a solo depresso-in-the-making but someone whose psyche will likely be poked and prodded from here on out by an army of professionals for years to come. Maybe someone will do a Rorschach on you. (Spend ten minutes describing each inkblot to ensure your test administrator doesn't think you're simple.)

It was in high school that I saw my first therapist. Not quite the experience I had been hoping for and looking forward to. She was very nice but seemed to think I was blowing things out of proportion. She felt that way, I realize now, because I never spoke to her in the stark language of depression. I wasn't someone who came in, slumped in the chair, and mumbled about wanting to die.

I was too caught up in my cloak of self-help language. She wasn't going to analyze me; I was going to beat her to the punch. It was a pattern I would repeat with therapists for many years.

The absolute worst therapeutic experience I ever had came when I decided to try a new technique, hypnotherapy. When I met this new therapist—we'll call him Cliff—I suspected I was in trouble just by the look of him.

Cliff didn't look like a therapist. His body hadn't withered away; he didn't seem to be living a life of the mind. Not that he was particularly healthy or fit. He just looked . . . regular. He had a slight paunch tucked into a Casual Friday kind of cowboy pants-and-shirt ensemble.

But I tried to keep an open mind. I started to tell Cliff about my history of depression, but before I knew it, he was interrupting me.

"Hold up a minute," he said. "People have a tendency to come into therapy and want to tell their story."

Oh no. I was going to have to prove my depression to a guy who probably once self-diagnosed depression but realized he had merely forgotten to eat breakfast and then decided everyone else who claimed to be depressed was, like him, being a bit dramatic.

He went on to suggest that people have narratives about themselves that they repeat over and over again, in effect solidifying them and turning them into self-fulfilling prophecies.

Ugh, this was *such old news* to me. He hadn't even been listening. I could tell because I had very deliberately just stuck to the facts, for this very reason, so as to carefully avoid "running a negative script."

Then, all of a sudden he clapped his hands together and said, "Bam! Now why'd I do that?"

I smiled politely. "To surprise me and jolt me out of an old scrip—"

But he wasn't listening and instead started to explain: "I did it to surprise you and jolt you out of your old script."

Good God, man.

I realized right away I was dealing with a Tony Robbins fan. I tried to jump in and explain to him—in the most delicate way possible—that I wasn't some idiot in a bad mood who was simply ignorant of the many mood-shifting strategies presented in the Personal Development section. I was trying to clue him in that his two-bit Tony act wasn't gonna work for me. But the dude could not take a hint. I even dropped a reference to Tony's work, to subtly alert him that if he passed off Tony's ideas as his own, I'd know.

He then got very excited that I'd heard of his King. "Look," he said. "I've done the Personal Power weekends, I've walked on the coals, and I've met Sage." Tony often has workshop participants walk across hot coals to prove to them they can do anything. And Tony's wife is named Sage.

I tried to shift the conversation back to my crippling

depression, but again he interrupted me: "What happens," he asked, "when a bike's chain isn't greased?"

Look, Cliff, I don't fucking know. It slips off the gear? It jams? It cracks? The fact is, I know what you're getting at, but I don't have the knowledge of bicycles to answer within your impotent metaphor.

I was completely unimpressed by everything he said and knew exactly what he was trying to do at every moment, and yet he insisted on interpreting the expression on my face as one of a closed-off woman shocked by his "unorthodox methods."

We finally got around to the hypnotherapy. He explained it to me slowly and idiotically like I was some bonneted Puritan afraid the therapy was actually devil worship. He said, "I'm not gonna wave a clock in from of your face or make you cluck like a chicken, and you will be in full control the whole time."

He said it as if women regularly lost control of themselves around him. Ew, Cliff. It was just like the time a young suitor warned me of his seductive abilities, saying, "Women have compared me to some pretty terrible but effective people in history." "So you're referring to Hitler," I replied. He looked impressed that I knew who he was referring to.

And the creepiness with the therapist only got worse. He told me to lie back on the couch and relax, so I did. But I felt weird lying there while he sat staring at me. I didn't want to self-consciously cover my breasts with my hands, so I left my arms at my side.

But then suddenly it felt like my boobs were resting on top of my body like two squat Cinderella pumpkins on a table.

How can I get out of here as soon as possible? I thought. I decided to just grin and bear it. The hypnotherapy exercise was over soon enough, since it was basically some deep breathing. I'd force a breath, and he'd say things like "That's a girl!" After it was over, I made up some bullshit he wanted to hear. He nodded and grinned maniacally. I went home and reenacted his entire shtick to my parents over dinner.

I feel bad shitting on Cliff, and I'm sure he was helpful to some people. But I felt like I was watching a new Cutco knife salesman pitch me the knives. A salesman who didn't know that I was the president of Cutco. Years later I ran into Cliff at the same therapy center, and he noted how radiant I looked.

The moral of my story is that as you enter this new wide world of therapy, remember that just because wisdom comes on the backs of fools and little children, doesn't mean you have to sit at the feet of every idiot you come across.

Okay, you may want to shell out for a few sessions with a fool or two, if only because afterward it will give you a brief but well-earned sense of superiority while you head home as depressed as when you arrived.

I've had some therapists who weren't as bad as Cliff, but instead of trying to challenge me, they've been overly charmed by my depressive wit. I get it. There can be something romantic, poetic, about depression, especially if the depressed person has a way with words. But really this doesn't do either of you any good.

If you want to make sure your doctor treats your depression as a pathology of the brain and not as the artistic creation of a young poet wrestling with the angels over life's mysteries, then you need to make sure you're not charming him too much.

One time a pretentious rodent I dated told me, "Your sadness is beautiful." Don't let your therapist misinterpret your depression as lovely sadness. It can be tempting to jazz up your stories. You're probably used to making your depression more palatable for others by adding a romantic detail to keep them from feeling too bad for you. But if you do this to a therapist who is starved for philosophical conversation, you might end up being encouraged to go off your meds.

. . . .

TOP EIGHT WAYS TO AVOID
CHARMING YOUR THERAPIST

1. Don't add romantic or artsy flourishes to your outfit on therapy day. No one is filming your session for HBO. If you are cold and going to wear a hat, do not don a beret. I know, it seems hard to imagine that clinically trained therapists wouldn't be able to see past your chapeau, but your serious expression, and tears, combined with that damn beret might bring them back to

their junior year abroad at the Sorbonne. They
might feel like they're in their favorite café with
that pensive Frenchman or little Edith Piaf again.
She really was a little bird, alighting near my American
member like a hummingbird to the sugar water.

2. Don't let any books of poetry go peeking out of
   your bag. If your therapist spots something he
   loved in college, you are in a danger zone.

3. Don't edit the gross details, whether emotional
   ones or physical. If you bled out your tampon on
   your rug because reaching for the cotton bullet
   or even shifting your hip position slightly was
   unthinkable, don't reframe it as "struggling with
   my moon cycle as usual."

4. No ironic insights or poignant details.

5. Do not quote song lyrics.

6. Avoid mentioning words like *god* or *purification*
   when talking about any form of self-harm, or
   your therapist might confuse you with a saint-
   to-be. I can't tell you how many times therapists
   have suggested that I might be meant for spiritual greatness.

7. Stop mugging. No facial expressions that rep-
   resent complex emotions. I find that too often
   a therapist's couch becomes a Mugs R Us, and
   suddenly I'm doing facial acrobatics I never do in
   my real life.

8. Really, stop treating the muscles around your
   eyes as a lyrical representational dance team.

. . . .

Whenever I found a therapist too delighted by me, I knew I had to get out. They were incapable of seeing past my charms and notions. I was like Woody Allen there. They couldn't have bathed in more aesthetically pleasing angst if they'd spent a night at the opera. I could see it when I looked up. They'd crack a smile and shift in their chair, like a favorite TV show has just come on.

If they had popcorn, they'd have eaten it. I would tease out the poetic details of a week spent alternately weeping, sleeping, and clenching my fists in my parents' house in a way that made it sound more like an Anne Tyler novel than a week of suffering on the wrong medication. They couldn't get enough of me. Then I'd have to go home and recuperate until next week's performance.

With one extremely expensive therapist, I attempted to drop the act and be as utterly boring as the depression was, flatly mumbling in response to questions about how I felt, things like "I don't know. I just . . ." She seemed appreciative of how much I was suffering, but she had trouble staying awake for it. Sometimes she'd start to nod off in her chair. I'd pretend not to notice, glance out the window, and cough to wake her up.

I love my current psychiatrist, the one who handles the meds. She's very alert but doesn't demand a show. In fact, she will usually laugh only during jokes I make at the end of the session, once the purse is on the shoulder. That's an appropriate way to shift from the graveness of the meeting to sending you out the door. Shuffling out, raising your gaze enough to meet the other half-conscious sufferers in the waiting room, doesn't really do much for anyone.

If you want to use your energy performing your mood, do it for the other people in the waiting room. These are the people to wear a beret for. When you enter, leave your shades on and pass time reading *Letters to a Young Poet*. When you head out, adjust those shades, and visibly steel yourself, pause before pushing open the door to the hallway, and head out of the waiting room, like a reluctant gladiator who has accepted his fate bravely steps into an arena. Set a pick between the next client and the door to the office, and maintain the block for as long as it takes to get through the first few lines of *Richard the Third. Now is the winter of my discontent.*

....

CHAPTER TEN

"COLLEGE," PEOPLE SAY. "THEY'RE THE BEST YEARS OF YOUR LIFE": PROVE THEM WRONG

Conventional wisdom says that kids who struggle to fit in during high school often blossom in college. The social hierarchy is less strict, everyone's a little older and more mature—and, of course, the kids are so psyched about being free of their parents and about the partying that awaits that they're often overcome by a newfound joy and openness, thanks to the Bob Marley poster hanging above their bunks.

At least that's how it's *supposed* to be. But what do you do when you still feel completely alienated from your newly exuberant, free-minded peers? I suggest taking up a cigarette habit and finding a friend who's as fucked up as you.

Freshman year of college at Georgetown University was pretty bleak for me. I can trace my unhappiness back to a single moment during orientation. People were gathering outside the freshman dorms. I remember music, lemonade, and dancing, which sounds like a bad party, but if dancing is how we show each other we have working pelvises capable of mating, I guess it makes sense.

A boy I'd met a few days earlier on a canoe trip for the incoming students called my name and gestured to me from atop a picnic table. He was gyrating boldly and waving his hands. He wanted me to get up on the tabletop and dance with him. I couldn't do it. I just couldn't perform that kind of exuberance. It wasn't me. Maybe if I had hopped up and started backing my ass up into his jock, things would have gone differently.

I did not, and that was the beginning of the end.

But luckily I came to have one very close friend in college. She was a girl we'll call Dawn, because that wasn't her name, but it suits her. We met in the waiting room of the student therapy center, so I knew there was a good chance she was a fellow depresso. The entrance to the building was the bottom of what everyone called the Rape Steps: an outdoor set of gently sloping concrete stairs, which rumor had it were designed in a way that favored the gait of a woman over the man who was chasing her. Something to do with physics, I believe.

Dawn and I immediately bonded as two Jewish mental cases from New York. Her main issues came from her severe ADD and related anxiety, for which she took Adderall. I don't know what I would have done without Dawn; she and I started hanging out constantly. She certainly was a reprieve from my roommate, a chipper former high school valedictorian who had no patience for me. I started sleeping over in Dawn's room, the two of us stuffed in one of those absurdly narrow Twin Extra Long college cots.

During the days, Dawn would straighten my hair with her expensive Futura hair iron. I'd straighten hers. We'd also apply elaborate eye makeup, and only then, feeling especially human, would we venture out of the darkness of our dorm to get sandwiches from the favored deli to eat on the lawn. But despite sitting in blinding sunshine and the outside-in theory of sprucing up your physical appearance in order to feel better, of course I remained depressed. It's kind of like how you think you won't be scared if you watch a horror movie during the daytime, but then you are. After all, a sun-dappled morning allows you to see a threat from far away. You sit in lengthy dread as a wounded monster crests the horizon, then drags himself along the pavement, turns, and rolls down your driveway.

At night, Dawn and I would stay close to the dorm. I'd sing Ani DiFranco songs to her, pausing to explicate the lyrics at the end of each verse before continuing. Each song took twenty minutes. We'd smoke a cigarette or two every half hour, and I'd order Philly cheesesteaks to the dorm. Those and cigarettes were the only illicit substances I dabbled in at that point, but that would soon change.

One time, we sat in a study group in the library, comparing neuroses. We talked about everything, big issues like depression and ADD, and then the subtle brush strokes of our experience, like my inability to imagine biting into popcorn without then picturing a hair tangled around the kernel, or Dawn's intolerance for anything touching her neck. A fellow classmate even commented, "Wow, this stuff's really real to you guys."

We looked at each other and laughed, shocked at how it was *not* real to him.

....

CHAPTER ELEVEN

ALCOHOL AND DRUGS:
FIGURE OUT HOW SELF-MEDICATION FITS INTO YOUR LIFESTYLE

While I did some occasional drinking in high school, college is, of course, when everyone becomes true lushes. Even then, it wasn't really for me. I often noticed that I would feel especially depressed a couple days after I'd had more than a few drinks. This kept on happening, so I decided to abstain.

It really goes to show how depressed I was: sobriety is a bold choice for a college student.

Smoking cigarettes, on the other hand, seemed like a good thing for my depression. It forced me to go outside at regular intervals throughout the day. Every therapist I have ever seen has told me to get outside and breathe some fresh air, and you get lots of it between puffs of burning chemicals. In fact, if you have the means, I'd encourage you to go right now and pick up a pack. It's a great way to satisfy your suicidal impulse without immediate consequence to family and friends.

But beyond cigarettes and alcohol (oh, and my anti-depressants), I had little experience with drugs of any kind. I think this is because the depression got me so early in life that I was still under the sway of school-age antidrug propaganda. I truly felt drugs would only make matters worse.

And as you may have picked up, food is my preferred vice, and I have eaten pizza with an endurance, fortitude, and flair that you've probably never seen in a woman or other mammal.

In college, like most people at that age, I partook in occasional tokes and that one massive bong hit of marijuana that caused me to lose track of my limbs. I liked it okay, but, of course, marijuana is classified as a "downer," or a depressant, not exactly something I needed help with. Usually, it just made me want to go to sleep, which is what I already wanted to do.

One night, Dawn and I decided to experiment with crushing and snorting one of her Adderalls, which in case you don't know is basically a light form of speed. The Addy (as I'll admit we called it lovingly) pills are blue, which always made me think of them as a child's Flintstones Vitamins–type version of cocaine. I've never actually done cocaine, but I know it's white, because it's for adults and they don't need fun colors to inspire them to use drugs.

When you take Adderall as prescribed, the body breaks it down at a certain rate, helping you stay "on task" over the course of a number of hours. In theory. Whenever I take Adderall, I become suddenly obsessed with modular storage solutions. When you crush Adderall and snort it, like Dawn and I did, you experience eight hours' worth right away.

At parties I'd seen friends "bumping" (a term I found impressive in its elusiveness) the stuff, and on the one hand there was something awesomely raw and extreme about crushing and snorting something, like I had seen in movies. On the other hand, Dawn and I were just nerds alone in our dorm. It felt kind of tame, like two teens splitting a beer at their parents' house.

But it was a lot of fun and extremely effective in the short term. If my mood was a mouth, the Addy felt like swallowing a menthol lozenge. It blasted cold refreshment through unexpected passages of vacant darkness I hadn't realized were there. And then thirty minutes later, I needed more.

This experiment took place during the last few weeks of freshman year, when classes had ended and we had nothing to do but finish up coursework and prepare for finals. I had stopped taking any meds and was in truly pitiful shape. I knew I needed to be back on some kind of antidepressant but wasn't sure which ones, and so I decided I'd wait until I got home and met up with my old psychiatrist. I just had to survive the last two weeks of school, and fortunately Dawn had enough Adderall to get both of us through.

The Addy also had the bonus of decreasing our appetite, which was completely thrilling for a piglet like me. Dawn and I would go to the meal hall, feeling slightly nauseated, and get Caesar salads we barely picked at. It was an experience in itself to roam among the heat-lamp-lit vats of stews and lasagnas and not feel pulled to eat all of it.

Those salads, plus a small topping of greasy chicken strips, were all we ate for a few weeks while we sat around discussing whether or not the rumors were true: that school officials spray calories on the lettuce to keep the freshmen anorexics from losing too much weight. I think that was merely legend, because soon after, I remember noticing I had a flat stomach, and looking at it in Dawn's mirror I couldn't help but smile at the sight. We both knew it was wrong to enjoy the fruits of our drug use, but we felt that given all the suffering of our respective depressions, we were allowed to count the abs as a win.

The Adderall use culminated in an epically efficient and organized packing effort a week before I had to leave. My roommate was gone, and I neatly stacked all possessions and my duffel atop her bare mattress. There I lived like a thin soldier for a week. The strangest expression of my Adderall use was that I spilled a soda on the floor and let the puddle sit there, undisturbed for days, surrounded by perfect neatness. When my dad came to pick me up, I sopped up the soda moments before he entered the room. As a young depresso, fear of embarrassment could still inspire me into action.

That was the extent of my dalliance in the world of hard-ish drugs. I can only hope that you learn from my missed opportunities and participate in all sorts of reck-less, self-destructive drug and alcohol abuse through-out your college years. Not, of course, for the positive, social-lubricant purpose of bonding with your peers through typical college experimentation. But, rather, so that you can come at your burgeoning depression from yet another angle and give it the full range of unhealthy influences it deserves.

CHAPTER TWELVE

....

THE PHARMA SHUFFLE:
GO OFF AND ON AND OFF AND ON VARIOUS MEDS IN AN ENDLESS, SHODDY, POORLY ORGANIZED, BARELY CONTROLLED EXPERIMENT ON YOUR OWN BODY

I had been on some form of antidepressants since high school, but by college I had become an expert. My college dealer—or psychiatrist, if you want to use the clinical term—was Dr. Z, a Transylvanian who looked like an emaciated Anjelica Huston, but without an infectious laugh or powerful charisma.

But I respected her silence. After listening to a patient describe his or her symptoms, she wouldn't say anything; she'd just slide open her filing cabinet and hand over boxes of Zoloft samples.

Medication sample containers are always immense in comparison to the quantity of pills they contain. They're like billboard ads for the pill with one actual pill attached. So in order to get enough free pills to last a week, I'd have to carry ten Kleenex box–size samples back to my dorm, balancing the stack between my hands and chin, like Gus and his cheese* cubes. (Yes, you know him, you love him: the fat mouse in *Cinderella*.)

Other than the ridiculously humongous sample containers, the big problem with psychiatric meds, as you'll soon figure out if you haven't yet, is that they don't always work. The Zoloft I got from Dr. Z wasn't effective. And, as advertised, the meds often have side effects that can be unpleasant. I, however, maintain that side effects are an added benefit, the only benefit of a med that isn't working. Headaches and intestinal discomfort make for great relatable excuses for refusing to participate in some group trip to a shadeless amusement park. Telling people you're too depressed to go just leads to them evangelizing the mood-lifting effects of a five-hour van trip to Six Flags.

Not to mention, if you ever bring up in public the fact that you are on meds, you run the risk of having to listen to some asshole who doesn't believe in them, who thinks they dull the personality or are a refusal to truly deal with your problems. Or some BS like that.

I fully believe in meds myself (it helps boost the pla-

---

* Recently, upon referencing Gus's cheese cubes to a very slight friend, Cole, he gently mentioned that he recalled them to be bits of corn. I misremembered because I prefer cheese.

cebo effect), despite their unreliability and unknown long-term effects. My view is this: when it comes down to it, your entire physical being is no more than a stew of chemicals and hormones anyway, so why not tinker with the ingredients?

I've always thought of my body as a lab experiment, and it's worked well for me. Zoloft wasn't my favorite, but when I went home that summer after freshman year, my old psychiatrist started me on Wellbutrin, which was great. I committed to do everything within my power to feel better before heading back to school in the fall. I started eating a strict ratio of proteins, grains, veggies, and fat out of *The Food Bible*. I jogged regularly and even got a job at the swim club where some of my old friends worked as lifeguards.

I wasn't a lifeguard, of course. The idea of seeking out certification and possibly having to give a kid CPR was overwhelming. I was hired as a desk girl, which meant I sat in the parking lot at the gate entrance to the club. I asked the members their names, checked them off, and handled their guest passes. I also got to swim on my breaks and go there on days off. (Will I ever be a legitimate member of a club?)

The structure was good for me, both time-wise and because I got to have a chair and table. I even did some reading on the job; David Sedaris's *Me Talk Pretty One Day* was my best friend that summer. I had avoided the book for a while because I had no idea it was humor; I thought it was a sincere memoir, albeit one with an offensively insipid title, about someone who longed to one day speak well.

But once I started reading, I, like the rest of the world, loved it. Reading it at my desk accomplished the same thing as my old cubby and mouth productions, a sense of interiority in a place where I felt exposed. And I didn't even need my thumbs to play the roles of his mother and sister.

I also found solace in some of the people I saw on a regular basis at the club. There was a man who used to show up alone and do laps in the pool, but instead of swim, he would walk, incredibly slowly, down and back the lane. I felt a kinship with him, convinced he was suffering some kind of monstrous depression, too. I wondered if I should begin an affair with him. It seemed like good fodder for a small indie film I could later write.

By the end of summer, I was feeling significantly better but was nervous about heading back to school for sophomore year. I handled this by spending four hours at Bed, Bath & Beyond trying to find a perfect sheet and duvet set that would maintain my sanity in the hell zone that was college.

I specifically created a caffè latte of a bed with deep mochas and milky-tan linens. I had recently been harboring hopes that a college romance was going to save my life, and I believed florals might discourage my would-be Romeo from wanting to be in my bed. One of the lifeguards pointed out that if a guy wanted to sleep with you, florals wouldn't stop him.

I convinced myself this wasn't true in all cases, and that floral prints had indeed been the obstacle preventing my previous year's crush from staying over. I managed to persuade myself that this boy had been different from the others. And it turned out he was; he was gay.[*]

_____

* Update: not gay, merely raised in the arts, didn't love me.

....

CHAPTER THIRTEEN

SOCIALIZING FOR THE BURGEONING DEPRESSIVE:
OR, I HAVE NOTHING TO OFFER, SO I BROUGHT NOTHING TO THE PARTY

My cappuccino sheets weren't luring men yet, but by the beginning of sophomore year I was making a concerted effort to be more social and outgoing. It wasn't easy. College campuses are populated by an endless throng of happy, dancing, fully conversational creatures who seem to exist for the sole purpose of reinforcing your utter alienation. I tried to take comfort in the fact that, as I learned in philosophy class, hell is other people and ultimately we are alone anyway.

Needless to say, the depression I had managed to keep at bay during the summer soon returned with a vengeance. The novelty of fresh sheets had not been enough. I tried to think of home and the sunny days at the swim club. I also had "phoner" sessions with the old therapist from my hometown. To conduct these calls in relative privacy, I'd take my cell phone out on the stoop of our student apartment complex—cup of coffee and cigarette in hand, naturally—and proceed to give her my reports from the front lines.

One night during a call like this, I had been talking her ear off for about thirty minutes already, describing the latest drama with a romantic prospect, when she changed the subject and said: "So, any thoughts on what's happened?"

I wasn't sure what she meant. I responded: "Well, that's the problem. Like, nothing has. He hasn't texted back in, like, eight hours."

She then explained that she was referring to what had happened at the World Trade Center. See, this phone call was happening on September 11, 2001. Or maybe the next day. In any case, it was very, very close to 9/11.

I was embarrassed and scrambled desperately to make up an excuse. "Oh, right, right," I stammered. "I guess I'm just still in shock. I can't process it . . . we all handle grief in different ways. I mean, I did see *him* at a candlelight vigil, but I feel like he thought my insights on tragedy were lame."

Looking back on this now, I understand why I only wanted to talk about myself and my failed attempts to be more social and find romance. Like everyone, I was horrified by 9/11. But nothing about that kind of grief was pathological. It wasn't connected at all to my depression. And I didn't feel like using therapy dollars on parsing through *appropriate* emotions.

When things are objectively shitty, whether on a local scale (a death in the family) or global (bombings, starvation, nasty YouTube comment that rings true, the biggies), I process the events relatively smoothly. In fact, I'm always at least partially relieved to feel horrified or saddened in response to something that deserves it. There is a small pleasure in feeling a fully round tear escaping the surface adhesion of the wet eye to fall heavily, then thinking to oneself, "look at me, reacting like quite the human."

I don't feel I need to talk in therapy about a grandparent's death. I'd much rather discuss why my self-esteem is so fragile or why my feeble attempts at socializing with other college students are so disastrous. Or better yet, why, when a romantic prospect's text to me doesn't include an exclamation point where I feel it should, I fling myself onto the bed, unable to maintain the evolutionary gains made by the *Homo erectus* species over hundreds of thousands of years.

Trying to get the boy I liked to like me back, and failing, or trying unsuccessfully to enjoy a dorm party, was in some ways worse than just languishing in isolation. I remember one evening in particular I was in the student lounge, a large room filled with seemingly healthy*

---

* Like this one pair of gorgeous blondes, the first of whose palms later turned orange from only eating carrots in her desperation to achieve a thinness only the second blonde's slight bone frame could achieve.

students working and socializing. I was slumped low in one of those itchy wood-and-wool hospital chairs, alone but in close proximity to all the other students and their conversations.

I felt heavy and slow, disoriented and irritated, in what I learned a day later via Underwear Telegram was a state of wild premenstrual agitation. I recall feeling separated from everyone around me and having an epiphany that perhaps my best option was to drop out of school, move to Manhattan, and throw myself into something totally different, something visceral and artistic, specifically puppetry.

Keep in mind this wasn't totally out of left field. I had my elementary school under-the-desk thumb-puppet background. As a child I had also owned and cherished a Mexican souvenir marionette. Okay, it's not much, but it's as good a reason as any to pursue an art.

Also, I once read a theorist who said that women are only in their right minds and true selves when on their periods. So, I wondered, maybe these frenzied few days were the only time I was accessing truth. I must listen to the call of the puppets before the menstrual window closes and I return to sleepwalking in utter falsehood.

In retrospect, I see that my puppet fetish was a stand-in for the social interactions with other human beings I was missing. You could make puppets respond to you in whatever way you pleased. You were holding the strings . . . or remote controls. (I had some engineering ideas involving nano-robots.)

But, alas, my puppet career didn't take. For a few days, I was stuck on the idea that Big Apple hand-based acting was my one moment of clarity, and if I let it pass by I would be ignoring my true voice within.

Maybe dropping out of school and pursuing puppetry wouldn't have been the answer. But maybe it would? Maybe becoming a Henson disciple could have been a turning point, the bold choice that would finally allow me to become my true self and then find like-minded full-size others with whom to socialize for small periods before returning to practicing on a smaller version in animated felt.

I'll never really know. I suppose I didn't seek out a hearty group of buds because I actually didn't want to socialize that much. There's nothing wrong with that. I was more interested in this time of my life being like a young sailor's first big sail, or in *Little Women* when Jo goes off to New York. And on top of doing my own laundry and getting to classes, securing a bunch of lovable bozos to surround myself with just sounded too exhausting.

Threading a friendship between two people—both of whom wear heavy, elaborate personality coats—involves too many subtleties, too many decisions, too much fine detail work. I've always found a much better way to unclothe them and connect is to actually unclothe them and connect through swift shock-and-awe sex acts. It's a fast and effective way to break down walls.

It's like when a black-ops division uses sleep deprivation and other tactics to break their trainees down to nothing in order to build them back up as supersoldiers. A shocking, bold sexual maneuver brings someone into their base, bodily self, and if you're poetic enough with your caresses and language, even to a place of emotional vulnerability, from which it's much easier to begin a friendship.

People ask, "Can (heterosexual) men and women be friends?" Yes. If you fuck them first, really well in the beginning to hook them and then terribly later on to wean them off. Then you have someone to go to the movies and share popcorn with, without being afraid of feeling their dick among the kernels, sticking up through a hole they cut with a traveling X-Acto.

Depression can dampen your personality and make it harder to socialize, but you are probably still able to use your body as bait as long as it holds its original shape somewhat. Your genital fruit is fresh. Your mothball pheromones haven't switched on yet. And there are hoards of ashamed virgins who can't believe they didn't get the deed done in high school, literally wandering around stupefied nightly waiting for you to scoop them up.

....

CHAPTER FOURTEEN

HEALTHY RELATIONSHIPS WON'T SERVE YOU NOW:
SAD, DESPERATE SEXUAL ENCOUNTERS ALLOW YOU TO PRETEND YOU'RE NOT DEPRESSED, BUT MERELY STRUGGLING THROUGH ACT 2 OF AN INDIE ABOUT A YOUNG GIRL DISCOVERING SELF-WORTH

Yes, depression may lead you on occasion to take desperate romantic actions that aren't exactly self-esteem wins, but that's okay. Lots of nondepressed people do that, too. And any time you channel your depression into behavior that resembles what the functional people do, it's probably a good thing.

One night in college, I desperately needed a change of scenery. I just had to get out and go away somewhere. Depression has many tentacles, and if you are in your dorm room, the tentacles are probably knotted around your cheap furniture, suctions clinging to your elfa bins.

But the good news is that if you get up and leave, the giant depression squid takes a while to untangle and catch up to you.

In some ways, we all live on the run, right? Some people are on the run from the law, of course. That's standard. But others run from their demons. I'm not talking about their addictions or tragic memories. I'm talking about actual demons, like possessions and devil hauntings.

My intention was to go on the run and head somewhere alone, but I ended up bringing along a fellow. Our destination? A boutique hotel with a name like "The Flame." It wasn't a normal hotel. It was designed for the sole purpose of giving the nouveaux riche a venue for cheap sex.

I don't mean cheap sex in a monetary way, but in the sense of being very far from making love. Okay, all you really need to know is it was not a family-friendly destination. Everything from the lamps to soaps seemed to subtly be asking you to initiate ass play.

The boy I brought to this den of sin was a friend who I was always trying to seduce into loving me. When he agreed to accompany me to the Flame, I was thrilled. I'd have him alone and for a whole night.

My friend was drunk, he mentioned later. I was in a state of stupor, too, but just from not being able to get over my unbelievable luck. The gods were smiling on me. I mean, it's not exactly easy to get a college guy to agree to come with a girl to a hotel alone with nothing but the promise of sexual activity.

As usual, I spent the next eight hours trying to make him fall in love with me. But he, like a few key crushes before him, was unable to see past my desperation. People have such an unfair prejudice against the violently clingy lover. Just because my yearning is bleeding out of every orifice doesn't mean I'm not worth loving.

These boys never understand that once they agree to love you, you'll settle down like a puppy instantly aging into a dog. They have no vision. No faith.

Keep this in mind and don't feel bad if, like so many women, you are 100 percent sure that a certain someone will one day love you and just doesn't know it yet. Continue to sacrifice time, energy, and self-esteem chasing after crumbs of their affection like a church mouse on Monday morning.

We *are* 100 percent right. We are legion. One day we shall inherit the earth.

But for now, we sometimes have to settle, like I did, for cravenly throwing ourselves at the object of our affection. And that's what college is supposed to be about anyway, is it not? Romantic adventure, sexual thrill seeking. There's no such thing as prostituting yourself in college, because it's a free-for-all to begin with.

Not that prostitution is inherently bad anyway. In fact, to a depressive—someone who struggles with setting an alarm in the morning, getting out of bed and to a job—the "oldest profession" holds appeal. You can relate to this, no? Haven't you ever thought, *It sounds so wonderfully easy,* and then, *There must be a catch!*

And you'd be right about that. While making money on your back without leaving the home certainly sounds amazing—and you get to create your own hours—there's one huge drawback at the center of it all: bookkeeping. It can be very tricky as a prostitute to keep your personal expenses separate from your work ones. Who is the clotriminazole really for?

But that's the only thing holding me back. As a depressed and confused feminist, I resent the contemporary stigma surrounding the practice of prostitution. Back in the day, people surely respected hookers. They were just working women doing what needed to be done to pay for a room of one's own. These days, everyone expects you to "better yourself" and "get a college education," and for some reason people are suspicious of the decision to get paid for sex.

Back in, I don't know, Old England, people assumed that prostitutes were just born to be prostitutes. But the silver lining was you were free to be an especially interesting or clever prostitute without someone suggesting you get out of the biz and study economics instead. If someone invents a time machine and I am randomly transported to any era before, say, 1960, I will immediately open up shop above the nearest tavern.

I don't think I'd enjoy the sex, but that's the part of it that makes things interesting. The work would be unpleasant enough that you'd feel like you really earned the right to relax the rest of the day. 'Tutes don't punch a clock. They keep bankers' hours.

But getting back to college, yeah, prostitution is kinda beside the point. And when you think about it, sex in college is rarely about intercourse. There just aren't enough firm and roomy beds. There seems to be an emphasis on *oral* sex, particularly the blow job, which everyone appears to use as a power move to mean everything from to "dear God, make me your wife" to "I will not be ignored."

I view blow jobs in themselves as an opportunity to exercise the virtue of humility. It can serve as a rigorous spiritual practice for spritely young seekers, especially when performed regularly. All the major religions have some form of bowing down as an expression of reveling in your smallness in the awesome face of God. Why do you think the gods put genitals halfway down the body if they didn't mean for us to mirror this pious act in our sexual behavior?

You're probably too depressed to have meaningful romantic connections or relationships with your college peers anyway, so you might as well revel in sins of the flesh. Your generally reduced affect will allow you to easily play the role of dissociative sex addict, if that interests you. It can be fun to hum "Better Man" inside your mind and stare off dead eyed while partaking in sex with a trustworthy, respectful brand-new nonvirgin. He'll have no idea you've cast him in the part of "that bastard."

....

CHAPTER FIFTEEN

COLLAPSE DEAD AT THE FINISH LINE:
GET A JOB AND A LIFE AND THEN SELF-DESTRUCT OVER THE COURSE OF MANY MONTHS IN A PERFORMANCE PIECE CALLED "ACTUALLY, THE DEPRESSION WON, BUT LOOK, I TOTALLY GAVE IT A GO!"

College is meant to train you not just for future bedroom skills but also for a future career or something, and by graduation I had fully immersed myself in stand-up comedy and creative writing. I even forwent a year abroad to "get ahead" in my improv troupe. I was trying to give myself a serious running start in the arts in college so when I graduated I'd have enough momentum to avoid getting a real job. I had been warned that a steady living makes people so "comfortable" they don't pursue their art.

After hiding out at my parents' for what felt like an

appropriate postcollege jag, I decided that in order to become Steve Martin, I needed to live in New York City, not commute an hour and back by car to open mics I'd really like to be boozing willy-nilly at. To do that—see if you can follow the logic—I needed to have a job that would allow me to pay rent there. (It took my dad half a year of repeated explanations over Subway sandwiches to help me understand this logic.)

So I whipped up some spec ad campaigns and had a graphic artist at the local mom-and-pop photocopy shop place them on images. I'm particularly proud of a line I came up with for Subway's new toasted subs: "Quit Cold Turkey." I trolled Craigslist, got a job at a boutique ad agency in Tribeca, and then panicked. In fact, the weekend before I was set to start, I became convinced I was developing schizophrenia.

Looking back on that time—finishing school, moving to NYC, getting my first real job and semblance of an adult life—it would be easy to blame the following self-implosion on the natural horror of the corporate world. Going in to an office every day *is* undeniably terrible and soul destroying in every way for some of us, from the commute to the fluorescent lights to the fraying plastic smiles to the elevator conversation.

But to a depressed person it's like Dante's *Inferno*: everything overwhelming about life wrapped up in one. It's *all* the pressure of trying to live up to expectations of others, *all* superficial BS.

On the other hand, there's something almost reassuring about being hit over the head with everything you fear all at once. Maybe you can relate. Maybe you're in a situation like I was, working ten to six at a funkily furnished company—pounded-copper sliding doors and a decorative motorcycle. (I am aware that those hours aren't bad. But when depressed, any set times are oppressive.)

But there are some advanced depression techniques that I learned to master in the corporate world that have served me well ever since. For example, crying in the bathroom . . . a bathroom stall is the one place in a company where you can hide out and gather yourself, the one crumb of privacy you have left. Use it wisely. I liked to pretend the stall was my tiny apartment, and I'd hide in there like . . . a thumb puppet in a desk.

In addition to the art of the restroom refuge, I became a master at the unquestionable excuse. When you're depressed, chances are you're going to be coming in late, if you make it in at all. For some reason this can be a problem with your superiors. But if you're smart about it, you can get away with anything, at least for a while. When you're making an excuse—for being late, or really for any obligation that you fail to meet—the trick is to say something that *sounds* like you're referring to an abortion clinic visit but leaves room for interpretation. What are they going to do, ask you to clarify? It works every time.

Unfortunately, on one occasion I made the mistake of telling the truth, and it was bad. As is often the case, I had the best intentions. I knew I wasn't dealing well with the stress of my new job, so I went to bed early to get a full night's rest before work. Some people have trouble sleeping if they're stressed. They end up staying awake all night thinking about the tasks they have to perform the next day. Me, I manage to sleep, but fitfully, dreaming wild, tumultuous dreams that barely seem to reunify my psyche at all.

So there I was, deep in dreamland, fighting for my family's honor against a battalion of past lovers. The battle lasted for days, and in the dream I woke up and shared the dream with friends, not realizing I was still in it. I tried to write it down, certain it would make a great movie plot, but when I looked at the pen I discovered it was full of . . . ew, semen? No doubt a reminder from the subconscious of the potency of my literary potential.

Oh wait, no. Not semen, just egg white, implanted there as a message of love and rebirth from the Sultan . . . I recognize this sultan's face, he's a bartender, but in my dream he heads up the marketing division . . . of my elementary school.

I wake up, and this time I know it's for real. I look at the heinous digital clock with the big red numbers and try to understand what they mean. What is *5*? Is it morning or night? Maybe the Sultan has the answer. I better talk to the Roaring Brook School Marketing Team . . .

And I'm asleep again.

Later. What is *9*? Is it morning or night? It's dark out, but what season is it again? Even if it were nine a.m. in the dead of winter, it would still be light. So that means it must be nighttime.

I've been asleep twenty-eight hours.

The numbers on the alarm clock terrify me. Lying on my side, the digital numerals stack vertically, and I experiment with ways of making them less scary, like trying to turn them into stick-figure friends, using the colon as eyes!

Finally, I roll out of bed. Literally. Not trying to break my fall, but landing as hard I can tolerate on the wooden floor to jolt my body awake.

I wish I could say it was the first time I had resorted to the falling-to-the-floor trick. But waking up had been a challenge ever since I started the job at the ad agency. For a few weeks during this period, I took to eating my long-time favorite ice cream, Ben and Jerry's Coffee Heathbar Crunch* in my morning shower, straight from the pint: nothing but the combination of hot water on my face and body contrasted with the blast of cold sugar and dairy could get my motor going.

Sometimes I'd leave the spoon there by accident, next to the shampoos, for my roommates to discover, which was not only deeply embarrassing but may have

---

* This flavor is now called Coffee Toffee Bar Crunch because Ben & Jerry's is "committed to using non-GMO ingredients," and Hershey's is not. Sadly, the new version gets a Novakian Thumbs Down, and I'm petitioning to bring back the GMO.

also led them to believe I was employing utensils in bizarre sex acts.

Needless to say, my two roommates at the time—two guys, Sam and Nedim—were accustomed to my odd behavior. Sam knew something was up with me but seemed slightly amused by my mishandling of life. Nedim and I had started off on a good foot, but it was probably a mistake that on the first day I lived there I made coffee at six a.m.—it gave him false hopes of what kind of roommate I was going to be.

Then there was the time I had left dishes in the sink. One of many times, but on this occasion, I knew I needed to handle them, but I physically couldn't leave my room. So I typed a letter of explanation, took a few steps to lean out my doorway, and slid the note under Nedim's. He later pointed out I could have just cleaned the dishes in the time it took to type and print the letter. He was right, but also wrong. Depression can be selective in what it finds tolerable. Standing, water, kitchen? No. Typing, crafting sentences, locating the printer cord, fishing out the trapped paper, printing, folding, and delivering? Yes.

And now, months later, here are Nedim and Sam again having to deal with my baffling behavior. They look up to see what caused the noise, the big thump on the floor, and I emerge from my room like a vision from hell: eyes swollen, face puffy, and limbs not yet reminded they're built for controlled movement.

"Oh shit," says Sam. "Have you been here all night?"

He's sitting on the couch, eating chicken, and binge-watching *Lost*. Eating dinner, watching TV. Normal shit. People tethered to time. How do they do it?

"I've been asleep."

"So I'm assuming you didn't go to work today?" asks Nedim.

Oh, that.

Then I go e-mail my boss, the creative director at my ad agency, and I cc the copywriter, who is also my superior. But for some reason, on this occasion, I can't bring myself to drop any hints about Planned Parenthood or a funeral home or any of my trademarks. There's no excuse, only what happened.

"I've been asleep for twenty-eight hours," I type. "I am sorry for the inconvenience this has caused. I didn't call because I was asleep."

I click SEND.

You already know what happened after that. My subsequent firing was a turning point in my life and my depression. I went back to my parents and moved in to my childhood bedroom. I basically retreated into a safe domestic world and began a passionate relationship with my bed.

In a broader sense, it represented a fundamental failure, but one that caused me to get real with myself. I had failed dramatically, not just at becoming the woman I always imagined when I was younger—supporting myself while making moves toward achieving my dreams, a Manhattan apartment, the whole fabulous facade—but also at *keeping my shit together* in the way I thought I could, being able to survive the corporate hell zone where I spent my days and having a handle on my depression.

For all you young readers who think you're gonna outrun your depression and close the door behind you as you reach adulthood, well, go for it. That hope might be what gets you through high school and college. But getting a job and living on your own, when your life is truly yours to make or break . . . that's where the depression will find you again if it hasn't already.

But if you do what I do, you can avoid complete despair and devastation. It's all about expectations and perspective. Yeah, you failed. But, hey, you gave it a shot! You told yourself you weren't going to let depression bring you down, and now, well, it brought you down. You took a few swings. So what are you going to do? I say you might as well go down easy and let it swallow you whole. You've finally reached the point where you are legitimately ready to push the pause button on life and just be.

PART THREE

HOW TO
BECOME A DEPRESSED
GROWN-UP

Once I moved back in with my parents in my early twenties, part of me wondered why it had taken so long to make the awesome realization that home is actually pretty great. Your home (or rather your parents' home) is your castle, and in the medieval sense that castle would have been your inheritance. The negative spin on moving back in with your parents is nothing more than an idea being pushed by Big Real Estate, and we must pay no more attention to its attempts to shame us than we do ads by Big Douche.

There is something beautiful about living entirely inside a protected domestic oasis. Adulthood has become too demanding. And, honestly, the outside world is overrated. "Growing up and leaving home to start a life" is such a 1950s concept. We could be the generation that pauses that endless building out, letting the world's resources buffer, while we replace our parents without growing beyond them. Depression makes it so hard to maintain this annoying lifestyle that you're meant to be a leader in the resistance. The moment you stop running from depression, you can do what I did, and give up, give in, and *go home*.

If at all possible, you should try to move back in to your childhood home, assuming it still exists. It will make you feel supremely disconnected from your adult life. Even if you're only making a brief foray into depression, consider at least making a visit.

And if you do move in, leave your adult possessions behind; let them languish in boxes in a basement or another facility. Seeing your prized Anthropologie mug is the last thing you need right now. It will just remind you of the life you've given up. It might even inspire you to get a new place on your own, which would defeat the whole purpose of pressing pause. The idea here is to bring your adult life to a *dead halt*.

If your childhood home no longer exists, you should move in with your parents wherever they may be, even if it's one of those assisted-living facilities. You want to fulfill your regression to a childhood identity by any means necessary. It'll give you a chance to try to grow up again, better this time.

If your parents are dead, see if you can move in to some other child's bedroom. Maybe you have a niece who's away at summer camp and you can stay in her room? Bonus if she has lots of stuffed animals to snuggle with—although I have found as an adult that stuffed animals are too lightweight to give you the same satisfying feeling of pressure from another's body.

....

CHAPTER SIXTEEN

HOME IS WHERE YOU CRY THE LOUDEST:
THE DEPRESSIVE DECORATES

The depressive's home is a sanctuary, and it must be treated as such. Just because you are depressed doesn't mean you don't care about your surroundings and your living situation. On the contrary, this is your chance to make your (parents', friend's, state hospital's) home your own, a place that doesn't demand you be anything but your perfectly diminished self.

If you're feeling semi-mobile, take every opportunity you can to redesign your living quarters now. The guiding principle here should be ease of use. You want to make your home energy efficient, not by building solar panels or any of that nonsense, but by conserving *your* future energy.

A good way to begin is to imagine you are decorating your home for a series of hypothetical characters, all of whom possess even less energy than you do:

First, envision someone who's ninety-seven years

old ... not a healthy ninety-seven-year-old, of course, but a true spokesman for decrepitude.

Next, take a look at some medical supply websites that specialize in elderly care. There's a whole world of cool stuff out there. Shower chairs, for example, can bring a new degree of ease and functionality to your daily ritual.

But why not take it to the next level with a full shower *bench*? According to one such site, a bench is "perfect for people concerned about stepping over the tub wall." The question is: who *isn't* concerned about this?

Or check this one out: grab bars. They "offer security to people needing help rising from a sit to stand position after using the toilet." Brilliant—Allegro Medical does it again! But I say why limit it to bathrooms? I suggest affixing bars to every wall in your house. Do it now, before your mood enters its next down cycle.

I understand it may be too much for you to handle to put yourself in the shoes of someone on death's door. If that's the case, you could try picturing someone who's not so old but maybe has two broken legs?

But honestly, who are you fooling ... it would take way less time for leg bones to heal than for your depression to go away. So forget about the broken legs. What's something even more crippling in the long term? Maybe a hip fracture?

I know from my research that people healing from a hip replacement sometimes use an elevated toilet seat because it's hard for them to lower their bodies. Don't dismiss an item like this just because you're currently able to bend at the waist. It's never too early to start conserving energy.

I even purchased a bed wedge recently. I use it as my pillow, and it makes it easier to get up after a nap. Instead of having to sit up ninety degrees, I only have to move forty-five degrees to be fully vertical. It may seem like a little thing, but it adds up. I'm saving myself hundreds of vertical degrees a week, and you can do the same.

But if you really want to go for it, I say imagine yourself as a French existentialist, someone who has given up on meaning (because he is French), but not his taste for rich sensual pleasures (also because he is French). A man like this might inspire you to keep some snacks in the bathroom. You already know I'm a fan of ice cream in the shower, but sometimes I also enjoy eating crackers there. It's exciting, like a race against time to gobble them up before the steam softens them to pulp.

Hot drinks in the shower are also excellent. You can be like a jar submerged in water, hot liquid warming you from the inside and out.

Whether you compare yourself to Sartre or to a frail old man or simply to a future elder-care technology innovator conducting research is up to you. But whatever you do, don't forget about the most important thing—casters. That's right, casters: the wheels on the bottom of furniture. Attach them to *everything*. Gone are the days of having to shove. A simple push of the pinky finger will send your desk flying.

And if it rolls too far, you can simply push yourself off the wall with a pinky as well. Your chair, of course, should be on casters, too. Rolling chairs are the original castered items, and I don't know why people stopped there.

And this book. Put it on casters and use it as a rolling snack tray.

And make sure to make the most of your bed. The bed is probably the most important of all. If the home is the depressive's castle, the bed is the throne. You will be spending a great deal of time there. Do whatever you can to turn it into a self-sustainable living center. This doesn't mean your bed has to be clean, but it has to be functional to a T.

Cleanliness is in fact much less important when you're depressed and spending all your time in bed. You don't need to worry nearly as much about linens. I mean, it depends on your body type. If you're a sweating beast or currently coaching an athlete's foot, I guess you'll have to wash your sheets regularly. But honestly, those sound like the kind of problems that afflict the more active set.

You're probably more like me: nice and dry, a potato with ideas. Which means your sheets won't get soiled by your body. Of course, you still have to deal with spills, but those go away if you ignore them. I think they call it "drying," but for all intents and purposes it's "disappearing," especially if evaporation is involved.

There are a handful of liquids that *will* soil a bed, but that still doesn't mean you have to clean it. Take coffee, for example. I spill coffee in bed all the time—often the entire mug. This usually happens when I bring a cup into the bed in an attempt to ease the transition from sleep to waking life.

I'll have a few sips and then nod off again. Then, when the mug slips from my hands and scalding liquid flies everywhere, I wake temporarily, scream once, and fall right back to sleep. Usually all that remains upon second waking is a faint smell of coffee, which is nice, kind of like sleeping in the mountains of Colombia.

So that's coffee. But then there are people who've soiled the bed with their bodily waste. That's never happened to me. But if it happens to you, don't worry. You're not alone. Look at drunk people. You often hear drunks talking about pissing the bed, and the reaction to such an admission is nothing more than laughter and hearty recognition. So if you piss yourself because you're depressed, you're really no worse than a functioning alcoholic.

And think of all the celebrated alcoholics, from Winston Churchill to Ernest Hemingway. They probably voided in their sheets because they lost control of their bladder, while you, my friend, soiled your linens as a purposeful outcry of objection against life. Yours is a bold urethral wailing, almost revolutionary.

But before we move on, we must consider one last example: crumbs.

You may think crumbs are intolerable in your bedsheets, even when you're depressed. I'm with you here.

May I suggest ordering online a small handheld vacuum to keep under the covers. If you'd rather not, consider the idea that crumbs might be useful. In eighth grade, that crabby Math 8A (*A,* I tell you!) teacher told us that Pythagoras or some such fellow used to eat crackers in bed because the resulting crumbs agitated him in a way that stimulated his brain. Thanks to his cracker habit, we now know about right triangles.

So don't leave the Nips in the kitchen out of fear. Maybe the remnants will tickle you into the invention of an essential mathematical theorem, or a plastic tampon launcher that doesn't have a claw at the end.

And if you absolutely must change your sheets, what-ever you do, please don't wash your old ones—get new ones delivered. Spread the new sheet on the bed, lie on top of it, then hire people to pull the corners down around the mattress. If they seem distressed about your role as a "sheet weight," remind them that you're paying them, so it's really not their business what you do.

Even better, don't pay them at all. My friend used to call upon submissives to clean her apartment—you know, those people who enjoy doing stuff for others with no reward or acknowledgment. Do *not* go feeling bad for them, or offering them a tray of lemonade. Just ignore them—that's what they want.

You win again, depresso!

....

CHAPTER SEVENTEEN

DO YOUR CRYING
ON A CAT:
CURLING UP IN THE
COMFORT OF PETS

When you're at home on your soiled bed, or on the floor, or in any corner of your abode where you're going to be spending a lot of time crying in a fetal position, you may want to bury your tears in the warm fur of a pet animal. I am partial to felines. So was Freud who said, "Time spent with cats is never wasted." This is good news for you, because spending time with a cat might be the only thing you do.

If you don't currently own a cat, use whatever on-line services necessary to get yourself one, or ideally two. Trust me, cats are so easy to care for that even you can do it. And a cat might just save your life. Then you can write one of those touching books about how a cat taught you to love again, and it will become a major best seller and a wholesome relatable actress might even star in the film.

There are plenty of best-selling books about dogs, too, and if you're more of a dog person, that's fine. I love dogs, even the ones I force myself to admit I don't find cute. Every day I come across dogs whose simple alert faces, bent ears, pert tails, and military trots create a feeling of love in me so profound the only response that seems suitable is gentle violence. I'll find myself wanting to pick him up like a furry football and dropkick him a thousand yards, where he'll land on a mattress of moss. You know, those specific acts of obliteration that cuteness calls for. Usually I just make a grunting sound, and say, "Cuuuuuute."

While dogs are great for streetwalkers, nothing compares to a cat for a depressive. It could be a kitten, an adult cat, or a geriatric old fuzzball. In fact, all three options have their advantages.

There's something about a baby meow artist that gives great pleasure to a depressive. The tiny fur form darts around the room as if a part of your soul, your own life force that has gone permanently missing. You wake up and feel a bit of your furry spirit sleeping on your face.

An adult cat, on the other hand, is more than just innocent kinetic life force. It has an already established personality, a fact that should inspire you. (Do *you* have a personality? Somewhat doubtful.) And if the cat's been living in a shelter, it will be impressed by your home, no matter how small, messy, dingy, and despairing.

Now, if you wind up with a geriatric cat—cats are

considered senior from anywhere between seven and ten years old—you'll have an entirely different set of circumstances to look forward to. It's hard to get older cats to eat, so vets suggest letting them nibble on whatever they want. This is great for the depressive, because you'll have license to share your food with them, in bed.

My cat, Blossom, aka Snook or Snoozer, lived until she was twenty-three. That means she was considered elderly for more than two-thirds of her life. But it didn't stop her from being a pro snuggler who could nap with the vigor of a kitten.

She was also extraordinarily wise in her old age, a small shaman who did healing work on whoever needed it. Despite the fact that her toothpaste was beef flavored, she was the embodiment of elegance.

All depressives should at least consider getting a wise, spiritually advanced geriatric cat. It's an easy way to be "of service" without moving much. The shelters are very happy when people adopt the elderly creatures.

A four-legged friend is, in my opinion, essential. I've even heard wonderful things about rats.

In general, six legs in a bed is better than two. Although, if I'm being honest, I tend to think of animals' front legs as arms.

And when you're on the floor, an animal won't be remotely disturbed. The two of you curled up in a fetal position makes for quite the sight. As I'm sure you've gleaned from TV and movies, this fetal position has long been the preferred one for depressed people—and for children hiding behind their slatted closet doors while their families are slaughtered.

If you haven't tried it yet, first you should attempt it solo, without a cat.

Trust me, now is the time. It's fun and there's a lot more to it than just lying there. There's a whole world of fetal-positioned activities that you've been missing out on.

For example, when the side of your temple is pressed against the floor—and only your one eye maintains a normal unobstructed view of the room—you can play a game in which you manipulate and distort the images in front of you. I've whiled away hours doing this, relaxing my gaze, allowing an object in my sightline to divide into two overlapping images, then collapsing them at varying speeds, honing my control.

Another fun activity is to picture yourself as an airplane with its wheels up. It may look like you're on the floor in fetal position, but really you're soaring to Paris. And your cat can do it with you. Imagine the two of you are Blue Angel fighter jets flying in tandem in a patriotic July Fourth display.

When I lived in New York, before I got fired, few people owned pets, because there's such a premium on space in that city. But the good news is you and your cat together in a fetal position take up so little room, you can both fit in a closet. Depressives already think of themselves as a "waste of space," so this aspect is important.

Especially if you're not planning on doing a lot

with your legs at the moment, or this year, you might as well save space and put them in a retracted position. It's more dignified than letting them swing around like baseball bats.

Of course, you'll want to uncurl occasionally to keep from atrophying. But whatever you do, don't arch your back in the other direction—it's been shown to combat depression. And it requires significant effort. The one benefit is it makes you look like the guy in that hideous early nineteenth-century painting of a tetanus sufferer featured in biology textbooks. Enacting scenes of medical horror can pass the time.

The only thing you must do is attempt a neutral spine once every few hours. This will allow the blood to flow to various extremities, but it won't thrust you into that "boy, oh gee, it's glorious to be alive" mood that might result from a Camel or a Half Wheel asana, or from throwing your arms up and back to conjure the sun gods.

Just lie long on your side, and see if you can get your cat to do it along with you. Think of yourself as a line segment, yes, a common line segment. When you don't believe you deserve to exist, reducing yourself to the space between two points is pretty satisfying. As a line segment, you're finite, two dimensional. You can be measured, your slope determined.

This is entirely different from being a vertical line, mind you. You may resemble a straight line-segment, but you're still horizontal.

When you give in to your depression and the pleasures of the home, you start to see yourself as a predominantly horizontal girl or boy in a vertical world. Being vertical comes to seem even more challenging than it once did.

This new identification with the X-axis will make it harder to stand up. You'll find yourself reflecting on Darwin and wondering whether humans evolving into bipeds might have been a mistake. And you'll start relating not only to cats and dogs but also to snakes and amphibious legless creatures. You are earth-bound like them. You are horizontal, stable.

Whereas moving through the world vertically feels like getting fire-hosed, like all the surface area of your body is being hit at once, when you're horizontal—prone on the floor or the bed, just you and your cat—it's like you're on the beach, the tide of life slowly coming in, with your feet out in front of you, so that only your toes run a risk of touching cold water.

When Quint, that grizzled fisherman from *Jaws*, gets eaten, his feet get taken first, then his knees, then his torso . . . it's a slow process during which he can come to terms with the idea of dying painfully on the open water. Gruesome, but at least he has time to adjust. It's the same with depressos. We choose a slow horizontal suffering, that we can ease in to, over quick vertical relief.

Vertically, everything hits you all at once. You walk into a cold wind, a new job, or a Starbucks where you recognize an acquaintance, and your entire front half is clocked with such force you might topple over.

Vertically, you feel vulnerable but also confined, pushed on both sides by time, like a bookmark stuck between the tightly folded pages of what's ahead and behind you. That's not a lot of room to exist in the now, folks.

But horizontally, you are an embodiment of the pause. In fact, you have not only stopped time but, in a way, gone back in time. By curling up in the fetal position, you have become, in effect, a giant baby.

It's kinda cute: a full-grown human trying to backpedal through the years of this endless promise-laden infomercial that is human life until the gods suck you back up into the great womb.

Maybe there'll come a day when you're equipped to race around in the fast-paced world of vertical living, but for now, allow yourself to relish in the horizontal. There'll be an opportunity later on, when you are a raging success biting your way through the wind, face-first through life, and your horizontal past will make you more compassionate. Maybe you'll need a file pulled for you by a poor intern, and when he fails you, you will show ... not mercy, no, you'll fire him, but you'll have the kindness to eat him feet first.

But for the moment, just take the time to master the poses I have taught you. You'll need them when it's just you and your cat on the floor, day after day. I know this fetal image may sound like a cliché of a depressed person, but remember, clinical depression is a disease and diseases have typical symptoms. You've earned the right to be typical. Lung cancer patients don't hold back their coughing because they're worried about people accusing them of overplaying it. *We get it, Don, you're dying.*

. . . .

TOP NINE THINGS TO LOVE ABOUT THE FLOOR

1. It's the king-size bed . . . that never ends. It feels good down there, right? No, nothing feels good, I know. Sorry.

2. But at least you can't fall any farther. That's the good thing about the floor. Unlike the figurative Rock Bottom, which can always get lower, the actual floor tends to stay in place.

3. When walking feels like swimming through a viscous ocean, and standing feels like treading water, the floor isn't just a floor: it's a life raft. It's extremely sturdy. You can stretch out. You will not drown.

4. In case of fire, you are less likely to die of smoke inhalation than your neighbors who are up and about. You won't even have to stop, drop, and roll. Just roll.

5. Because it's less comfortable than the bed, you can pat yourself on the back for roughing it. Lying in bed might be pure laziness; camping out on the floor is virtually an action adventure. Try mumbling something like "This op goes side-

ways in Tangiers, the boys at Langley will have me up to my tits in paperwork for the next two years."

6. Plenty of healthy people purposely lie on the floor. There are yoga studios full of people who pay to do it. Some yogis say Corpse pose is the most important one to master. So "breathe into it."

7. Take it a step further and really pretend to be a corpse. You're 90 percent there as it is.

8. Consider this: when you do become a corpse, popular opinion says you're not there to experience it, so this is really your only chance. For fun, think of something that really bothers you, then try "rolling over in your grave."

9. So if you're at home on the floor, you should feel legitimate in just staying there.

. . . .

....

CHAPTER EIGHTEEN

YOU'RE A REAL DEPRESSO NOW AND YOU'RE READY FOR YOUR UNIFORM:
THE DEPRESSIVE AND FASHION

Is there anything more emotionally draining and mentally taxing than clothing? You can't put on clothes without making a statement. And I'm not even counting those pithy sayings quilted across the ass of a pair of terry-cloth shorts. The good news for you is that, since you're not going out of the house, the only person your outfit is "talking to" is yourself—so you can say or not say with it whatever you damn well please.

When I moved home to the suburbs, I allowed myself the luxury of wearing a uniform every day of yoga pants, ribbed tank tops from Target, and Gap zip hoodie sweatshirts. I got the same sweatshirt in a variety of colors, partly as an experiment in chromotherapy and partly so I wouldn't have to confront how rarely I did my laundry. I also found that wearing something sold by the Gap made me feel like a normal person, the word *normal* having become a high-stakes concept for me at the time.

If you are in your home depression phase, in your *own* home, appreciate it while you can. This is the one time you don't have to deal with the expectation of adorning yourself with an outer layer. In fact, this is the one time you don't have to deal with clothing at all.

That's right, nakedness in the home is a must. Not only does it feel liberating, it keeps you from dirtying your uniform and allows you to put off doing laundry for months at a time. When you live like this, free and nippled, like the day you were born, the only things that really touch your skin are your bedsheets—and you can wash those when necessary via delivery service.

Some of you may be thinking, *What's she talking about, clothing is not that oppressive* . . . that's fine. Substitute something common, expected, that depression has rendered un-doable for you (using human language to communicate, paying for things with money). The message should hold.

Clothing the body is exasperating and brutal. You know the expression "everyone puts on their pants one leg a time?" Well, some people might find that an empowering notion, but I see the prospect of *one leg at a time* as exhausting. You put one leg through a hole, and then what, you're expected to do it all over again? *Immediately?*

I have interesting news for you. I have a different technique entirely. It's called Putting Pants on One Leg at a Time, with a Half Hour Break Between Legs. You can adjust the break time as necessary. The point is, you're the boss. This is your life, and you have permission to interpret typical human laws however you wish.

Put aside the old way of thinking that tells us we have to look "normal" and our clothing has to be a *statement*. I reject this grammar metaphor. If an outfit always has to be a sentence, I say it's a prison sentence, a terrible punishment we are cursed to live out over the course of a day, or even a short trip for chunks of watermelon at the bodega.

I am a militant when it comes to my anti-clothing-as-statement stance. And you should be, too. May I suggest starting by boycotting underwear. Or at least boycotting our culture's obsession with washing it. I never wash my undergarments. When I run out, I simply haul myself to the Walgreen's subsidiary and buy whatever is left in stock.

A pair of new, fresh underwear is 100 percent better than an old one that's just been washed. There is a pleasure in fresh underwear that can't be beat, especially for the depressive. It's almost enough to give you a new lease on life.

The best option of all, if you can swing it, is still definitely to go without. *But what if I have roommates, you ask?* Okay, in that case, have you considered long skirts? You can sit down in those without much thought, and your roommates won't be forced to see your genitalia when you're sprawled out on the sofa.

Still not convinced on the nudity thing? Look, if you refuse to see how wearing clothing is one of the most oppressive human traditions, take a moment to consider Adam and Eve. According to the Bible, I've heard, once these two discovered the concept of shame, they took up wearing leaves. That, in my opinion, was their first mistake, not counting the whole fall-from-grace thing.

But getting back to clothes, it was only a matter of time after Adam and Eve were forced to wear leaflets before elaborations developed: loincloth, pantaloons, hoop skirt, the classic trench, the crisp white shirt—and even, eventually, costumes made to resemble the original leaflets.

I understand why Adam and Eve and those who followed the folksy duo wanted something to wear on their areas. But no, I don't think it was all about shame. I believe it was connected to one of our other most oppressive traditions. Sitting up.

Loincloths serve little practical use when you're standing, when genitals would otherwise enjoy the soft pressure of a gentle breeze. Nor do they serve much purpose when you're lying down with your private parts neatly sandwiched between your legs or resting atop your left thigh.

But sitting up is when unclothed genitals really eat dirt.

As you can probably tell by now, apart from being a proponent of the occasional loincloth in the sitting position, I am generally pro nudity in all its forms. But ironically, I like to wear articles of clothing in the one place where it's socially acceptable to be nude—the shower. I like to get in with a shirt or sweatshirt on. It's a way of easing in. I wait until my legs are nice and warm under the spray of water, and only then do I peel off my top and send it flying over the curtain rod as I lean my torso swiftly under the warm stream.

. . . .

TOP FIVE TIPS FOR CRYING IN THE SHOWER

1. Lie down. If you find yourself unable to stand up any longer because you just don't have it in you to finish shampooing, and you know all you are capable of is lying down where you are: GO FOR IT.

2. Don't worry about resting near the drain. It might be a little grungy where your hair has gathered, along with a stray cherry pit and other items too big to go down the drain. And you're often forced to rest against the browning edge of the shower curtain liner. But those unpleasantries are the last of your concerns.

3. Feeling that you don't deserve to spend time cramped and limp on the floor of the shower is natural, but it shouldn't get in the way of you actually doing it. It's one of the essential rites of passage for a depresso.

4. It's always comforting to make friends out of fixtures. My favorite is the circular metal fixture with the protruding lever for closing the drain, aka its nose, and the two screws, its eyes, creating my mute Pinocchio, in whose reflection I

see a distorted version of myself. Also, a row of shampoo bottles can look a lot like a dignified, stiff-shouldered security team, keeping watch for intruders while you lie there in peace.

5. Remember, you will one day look back on the darkest moments of your depression, and those crying-in-the-shower episodes will sing out to you, almost proudly, as if to say, "We were the worst!" Be glad to have them under your belt.

. . . .

I also like to put on as many clothes as possible before leaving the bathroom. I'm not talking about drying off and dressing like you're going out. Who do you think you're talking to? Neither of us is going anywhere anytime soon. No, what I mean is just covering up yourself and your wet skin with lots of crazy layers while still in the steamy bathroom so that you can make the trip back to bed without being as frozen and preserved as a *Homo habilis* discovered in the arctic ice.

You may not share my exact predilections regarding strange uses of clothing in the home, but I hope you are picking up on my overall point—which is that, as an adult depressive living in the pause of time, hiding out in your cozy domestic retreat, you can choose your own sartorial adventures. You've earned it. At very least, wear a bathrobe for a week straight. I want you to feel empowered in your slobbery.

I chose to order some nubuck slippers from L.L. Bean

to really take ownership of my new housebound life, and it gave me a sense of sheepskin-lined purpose.

. . . .

TOP FOUR PEOPLE WHO DRESSED LIKE SHIT AND NONETHELESS THRIVED

1. George Washington. When he wasn't on the battlefield, he wore fanciful custom-made purple hats. This was highly unusual, indigo dye was rare and expensive, and flamboyancy wasn't encouraged in generals.

2. Franklin Delano Roosevelt used to wear slacks dirtied with grass stains on the knees. You can't see it in the photos because they were usually in black-and-white. But he did. People attributed it to a lack of pretension and a willingness to get his hands dirty solving a problem.

3. Amelia Earhart. Earhart is known in retrospect for that floppy-eared pilot's hat, sure, but during her lifetime, news pieces often noted that she wore a wheat necklace. Yeah, you heard me. Spun wheat secured with knotting techniques and then sprayed with resins to keep it from becoming brittle. It was as thick as a wreath. People speculated that it was filled with smelling salts to keep her alert during flights.

4. It's time I revealed to you that the three previous examples are lies. But maybe you believed them

when you read them. This is a lesson suggesting that these stories might as well have been true, and it should inspire you to know that whatever you choose to wear can later be contextualized by historians and believed by fools.

. . . .

CHAPTER NINETEEN

....

EAT TO NOT DIE, DON'T NOT DIE TO EAT:
THE DEPRESSIVE CHEF

Even if you're withdrawing from life in every other way, there's one aspect of human existence that you simply can't avoid: if you want to stay alive, you have to eat. But you certainly don't have to *cook*. Luckily, there's this thing called "ordering in." You may be familiar with it. But you may still be clinging to the old notion that ordering in is a special treat, not an everyday thing.

Nothing could be further from the truth. Depending on how you do it, ordering in can be way cheaper than grocery shopping. Buying fresh produce to make a multi-ingredient salad is so much more expensive than having a salad made for you. Plus, you won't have half a tomato rotting in the fridge.

Just remember to keep a pair of shorts by the door so you have something to throw on before greeting the delivery guy.

When you're living alone, in a city, you should be ordering in breakfast, lunch, and dinner. It's a whole new world these days. Let go of the old order-in paradigm. Your parents probably never ventured beyond delivery pizza, but it's a different ball game now.

For example, did you ever realize that you might order delivery for dinner and include *in that order* something that will freeze or refrigerate well enough that you can enjoy it for breakfast, lunch, or dinner the next day? I'm not talking about leftovers! I'm talking about ordering something *explicitly* for tomorrow. It's exciting, like having a personal chef.

I've often wondered why more people don't do this, and I've come to the conclusion that it's because they assume they might actually make it out of the house before the next meal. Not me. I think of my home as a ship on the ocean. I don't know when I'll see shore again, and if a boat passes by and offers to throw some oranges aboard, I'm taking them!

I'm also taking advantage of all the side-order options while I can. Whatever you do, don't skip over side orders. You might even want to cobble together a meal from the sides. Sometimes you get the exact same thing, but at a better price than the regular meal. For example, you might see that a side of grilled chicken costs $3.95 and a house salad is $6.95, but a grilled chicken salad is $12.95! Most menus are not the mathematically congruent documents you suspect.

Cooking is not prohibited, but because it's a sensual, embodied activity, it might not be appropriate for Rock

Bottom. You might want to save that kind of rich, textured experience for when you return to the world. If you really feel like you must prepare your own meals, what you need to do is run out and get (order online) an electric kettle. This is an essential item for the home depressive. Especially if you have roommates and don't want to risk running into them in the kitchen, an electric kettle allows you to make soup in the privacy of your own room.

Yes, soup. Specifically the sodium-heavy, fatty-noodled kinds. For many depressives, soup is their whole form of sustenance. And why shouldn't it be? It's a delightful, easy way to eat. You don't even need a spoon. You can just slurp up the liquid like Oliver Twist. And then when you get to the end of the cup, a little tap is all you need to project the remaining noodles into your mouth.

Food that you can eat with the absolute minimum effort is a good rule of thumb. For that reason, I highly recommend straws for soups as well. The wacky-shaped, looped kind. Who says those are just for kids?

You might also want to consider adding some other dried foods to the liquid. Things like seaweed. Jerky. Basically anything that comes with a silica packet is good.

Here is a great, all-purpose soup recipe for when you are depressed:

1. Boil water in your electric kettle.
2. Pour it into the cup of dried soup, aka Cup

Noodles, ramen, or a preferred artisanal brand if you're an asshole.

3. Don't rely on the paper lid to keep the heat in! It isn't, nor has it ever been, sufficient. Rest a book, maybe this one, atop the soup cup for a few minutes, and it will cook much better, faster.

4. Eat two and feel mildly satisfied.

If you really want to go buck wild and use a microwave but don't want to move beyond soup, consider nuking a glass jar of tomato sauce and then drinking it straight from the jar. Maybe add a little cheese. The sauce alone makes a great soup, and if the salt content is high enough, it will run right through you and give you a nice colon cleanse.

One thing to beware of, however: when you cook a tomato, it releases lycopene, which has antidepressant qualities. So don't hit the sauce too hard, if you know what's good for you.

....

CHAPTER TWENTY

COZY UP AT ROCK BOTTOM WITH A GOOD BOOK:
THE DEPRESSIVE READS

Once you've established your new lifestyle, you might need an activity to occupy your time. Now I know what you're thinking. *Books are work. Pressure. Why would I want that?* I get it. Books don't always cut it. And it takes energy just to hold up the book or e-reader and drag your gaze across the page again and again. Reading a line of text without slipping to the one below it can feel like a tightrope walk.

On the other hand, you're going to be spending a lot of time hiding out in bed, sulking under the covers anyway, so you might as well give it a shot. Who knows, you may find yourself transported through the magic of fiction to a different and wonderful new parallel reality!

. . . I don't actually believe that. I think the promise of escape through novels is a falsehood. If reading *actually* transported you, that would be something. But no, it's not like that at all. The burden is still on the reader to do all the work. Authors demand you use your own imagination to call up the images they've merely suggested. It's a nervy thing to do.

It's almost like these authors are taunting us, trying to get us to use our imaginations on purpose. It's kind of rude, no? Aren't *you*, Sir Author, supposed to be the one entertaining *me*?

Maybe on occasion I've felt transported to a different world while reading, but the feeling only lasts a few seconds, or if you're a bit of a weirdo, minutes. As soon as you look away from the page, you're back in the real world. You can't exactly *set up shop* inside Tolstoy's St. Petersburg or V. C. Andrews's bayou.

They say using your imagination is the whole point. It's what makes reading magical. Their argument is that however you might picture Stephen King's monster is even worse than if he showed you a drawing, because you unconsciously access the imagery that terrifies you most.

This effect proved true when my aunt Shira was a little girl, though with dreaming not reading. She woke up screaming in the middle of the night. When her mom and sisters ran in and asked what was wrong, she said she was having a nightmare in which Elsie the cow was tickling her armpit. Sounds delightful to us, sure, but in the language of her mind, it incited terror.

Fiction writers are hoping that when they say "monster," you'll fill in the image of Elsie tickling your feet.

They're *capitalizing on your demons.* They're as bad as therapists.

The other problem you'll run into in literature is that authors expect you to know words you don't. Some of the greatest writers have the completely annoying tendency, for example, to describe shrubbery and plants by their scientific name instead of just telling us what they look like. Honestly, how many among us are horticulturalists? Are these writers trying to flatter us by acting as if we were all classically educated in plant life?

This assumption by writers that we all grew up gardening and landscaping is both pretentious and offensive. I'll tolerate "the flat, wide leaves of the maple tree," where they teach you about the object as they name it. But to straight-up say, "The house was flanked by pachysandra"? That's rude.

You'll also need to watch out for concerned friends bearing books as gifts. Sometimes these books will appeal, but it is rare. My friend Ashley lent me her copy of Hermann Hesse's *Narcissus and Goldmund,* saying she thought it might speak to me as it did to her. And it did. In tongues.

I was hooked when I saw the tagline: "a raging battle between flesh and spirit." That is one of my favorite themes. It strikes at the heart of all human suffering and underscores perfectly the war waged deep in myself when deciding whether to retrieve popcorn from the lobby in the middle of the movie or just wait and go straight to dinner afterward. And frankly, why can't I do both?

This is usually when the battle evolves into flesh versus flesh—do I want classic old popcorn, or should I go for it and try the nacho cheese box? Something about flimsy cardstock food containers, held together entirely by their own origami, calls to me. I think the thrill lies in the fear the origami won't hold, which encourages me to quickly lighten its load.

All of which is to say, the themes of *Narcissus and Goldmund* feel relevant to a depressive like me. And the title is sure to impress anyone who happens to catch me reading it. *Narcissus* makes one think it might connect to mythology, and *Goldmund* simply sounds dignified. Is anyone named *Goldmund* anymore? What about *Rosamund*? I've noticed a distinct lack of *-mund* names in my lifetime.

But names aside, my friend was right: the book did speak to me ... at least until I tossed it aside halfway through. It was a risk, though. You never know how your depressed self is going to react to a work of literature. Even art that you enjoyed at one point in your life can take on a completely different cast when you are depressed.

If I am merely floating in the depression, but still with my head above water, I like to turn to poetry. The right poem can be a pulley device to hoist myself a few feet above the surface, where I can breathe without inhaling mosquitoes. But if I am drowning in the swamp, the same poem I once loved can become a flimsy mockery, dangling out of reach.

This happens to me every time with T. S. Eliot's

"The Love Song of J. Alfred Prufrock," which is one of my favorite poems (I know, it's everyone's favorite poem) when I'm feeling relatively good, when I'm able to access that winsome awe at the large and small of life.

But try reading it when you're depressed. I had no patience for this dude . . . enough about you daring to eat a peach, T.S.—who *hasn't* eaten one? And enough of your damn measuring out of life in coffee spoons. Sounds lovely, but we don't all have tea served up by our wives in the afternoon.

And what's all this crap about mermaids, Eliot? First, you make me feel like mermaids exist, and drinking coffee will make them appear, but moments later the poem ends and I am left with a gray sea, barren of mermaids, mermen, or anything legitimately fuckable by humans.

Where's Daryl Hannah when you need her? Which brings me to . . . movies. Movies are arguably even better than books when you're depressed. You don't have to exert the energy of moving your eyeballs from left to right. And they don't lay that whole burden of imagination thing on you like books do.

The chance that a movie will "transport" you is definitely greater than it is with a book. For example, you may be home depressed, but by watching beach-y movies in the comfort of your dark living room, you can have the best of both worlds—not have to go outdoors but still feel a six-pack-based kinship with the well-bronzed protagonists.

During the time I was living at my parents' house, I

was particularly fond of watching scary movies. A lot of depressives share this habit. I guess fear can be exhilarating and uncomfortable, and can give you a sensation of being "alive."

If you haven't yet grappled with the canon of terrifying films, I suggest you start off with the classics: *The Silence of the Lambs, The Shining,* or that tits-based film with the girls at summer camp . . .

Then, after you get through the film school syllabus, navigate your streaming service to the thriller section, and dig in. Next, work your way toward true crime. It's even better: it's all about the constant threat of violence in the real world.*

If your tolerance to horror movies gets too high, but you really need something scary to penetrate your stupor, you can get the adrenaline pumping with one of my favorite mood scrambles: Open your front door and leave it ajar. Retreat to the bathroom. After a minute or two, return to the entryway, shut the door, and lock it. Now walk around your house, wondering if a stranger is inside.

---

* Begin with the works of Harold Schechter, the leading authority on serial killers. Flip loosely through his *A to Z Encyclopedia of Serial Killers* and watch to see which heinous detail calls out to you. Reading about the habits of Albert Fish, who practiced every single known perversion and then created new ones, can be quite invigorating.

··

PART FOUR

HOW TO TAKE YOUR FULLY ACTUALIZED DEPRESSION INTO THE WIDER WORLD ... AND (GASP) GO OUTSIDE

··

This is the part where it can get hard. At some point, you may find yourself thinking you're ready to leave the pause, turn the clock back on, and venture outside. But you'll want to be very wary of this feeling. Depression is an underworld you don't just leave early on a whim.

If you snap out of a depression all of a sudden—or even if you just think that's what's happening—you risk missing out on the very thing the mood gods intended you to find when they nudged you on this blue quest in the first place. Nothing of merit was ever won without suffering, as we know from Jesus and low-carb diets.

After my first year living at home with my parents, I had established a life, if you want to call it that, with Mom and Dad. I had accepted them as my "life partners." I had even vowed to exit life when they did, via suicide. They brought me into this world, after all. So it would only be right that I leave the same time as them.

It was at Halloween, my second Halloween at my parents', giving out candy to the kids and seeing the little ones with their futures wide open, that I started to wonder if I was ever going to leave. Would I be in a different place next year or was this it?

This train of thought led me to a realization that my depression wasn't going anywhere. And since I probably wasn't going to be committing suicide any time soon— via my one-sided pact with my parents, who were still in good health—it was time for me to start contemplating a return to the outside world.

I knew I would still be depressed, but I'd be living with the depression at my side. I'd probably have to take things slowly, with more self-care and forgiveness. I'd have to accept that I wasn't going to be the perfect person I once imagined. Oh well. That person would have been an unsympathetic dick anyway.

So I did it. I went outside. To the depressive, hell is fresh air. But there comes a time when you have to bite the bucolic bullet and leave the house. You will be heading out as a different person than you were when you went in, and in many ways it will be a lesser version of you. But in some ways, even with your depression and all your limitations and imperfections, the new you will be more-than.

You will now have the gift of being able to bring everything you learned at home out into the Great Wide Open. All the personal peculiarities you indulged—

drinking soup out of loopy straws or pasta sauce straight from the jar—are about to be unleashed on the world. All that crying you did? Now you can see what it's like to weep in public.

"I don't want people to see me weep," you might say. But you're missing the point. In fact, the only thing that draws attention to the tears is your attempt to cover them up or to keep them in when they're threatening to flow.

When you hold in your sobs, you disrupt your breathing. That leads to the loud hiccuping kind of crying, the sudden bursts of tears, and worse—the mucus. Then you start wiping your face. Ugh, never wipe your face. It's all that wiping and inhaling of mucus that gives you the red puffy face.

The trick is to do this instead:

When you feel like life is so overwhelming that you have no choice but to cry, simply stop in your tracks and bend over like you're catching your breath after a run.

Then, let the tears fall straight down out of your eyes to the ground. Aim for perpendicularity. Your tears will avoid contaminating your cheeks, and you will not have to desperately swipe at your face, which is what leaves the irritation and telltale red marks.

Consider enacting a few vomitous heaves. It may seem like extra drama, but people will assume you are merely hungover after some all-night rager you attended with your million friends, rather than standing alone in the street, sobbing into the sidewalk, watering the dried gum on the ground.

. . . .

TOP FOUR TIPS FOR
CRYING IN A RESTAURANT

1. It's all about the napkin. Holding it up to your face like you're permanently wiping hollandaise off the corner of your mouth creates a tear catcher only a few inches from your eyes. If you remain stone still and stare boldly in one direction—for example, at another table, or at a painting—most people won't spot the tears.

2. Your waiter will notice, of course, but a quick *I'm-not-choking* smile in his direction and he'll quickly scamper away. His tip is at stake, and he won't hassle you.

3. Bonus: you might secure a free dessert, which will be embarrassing but delicious. I've had everything from a bowl of ice cream to a stunning sculptural patisserie placed in front of my puffy face.

4. Unfortunately, if you prefer savory items—a cheese plate, for example—you're out of luck. Waiters almost never bring savory comforts.

. . . .

While the emphasis here is on hiding your crying, that is only because I want you to know it's possible to enjoy a kind of privacy while crying on the go.

The bolder realization, and one you will happen on

naturally if you cry in public enough, is that it isn't so horrible for people to see you crying. It's a good reminder to those who see you, who are probably stifling their own tears, that they're not alone in the human condition. To weep in front of strangers, it is a public service.

CHAPTER TWENTY-ONE

....

MAKE PEACE WITH SUNSHINE:
THE DEPRESSIVE VENTURES OUTDOORS

Whatever you do, you need to take baby steps when you go outside. Don't think you're suddenly Lewis and Clark. The outer world is a completely different animal from what you've been used to for the past few years. It may feel different to you now. Be prepared for disappointment.

Part of the horror of the outdoors is that it is so oppressively, well . . . itself. It's remarkably stubborn in its physicality and consistent in its humdrum phenomena. Whether you're in a small town or a big city, it's going to be a shock when you march outside. You'll find yourself assaulted by the regularity of nature and the physical environment, its sturdy features (*There's that tree, as usual*) and routine events (*Oh, surprise, surprise, a train is coming along the train tracks*).

Compared to you—your weakness, inconsistency,

and general ambivalence about living—the outside world is a big, predictable slap in the face.

And the true natural world—the wilderness, the changing of the seasons, the rhythms of the earth—is even worse. You could stay in your house for three years, and spring would still insist upon happening again and again, as if you hadn't even boycotted it at all. Flowers wouldn't even have the courtesy to look jilted.

Don't believe me? Go ahead. Go outside and see if some little flowers aren't waving their little petals in your direction.* Don't say I didn't warn you.

The outside world may just be too much too soon. May I again suggest taking up cigarettes? I've found that filling the clean air with your exhaled breaths of cigarette smoke goes a long way toward bringing you back from the brink when you're feeling oppressed by nature and its annoying naturalness.

And if it feels like too much too soon, remember to take it slow. There are some outdoor places that feel safer to the former home-depressive than other, more intimidating locations. You'll find that public spaces where you can feel anonymous—libraries, cafés, et cetera—are the least threatening.

Remember that it was only recently that you let go of the idea that the world outside your home was a total nightmare. Don't fool yourself into thinking you're ready

---

* Sure they look friendly, but, really, they just don't give a damn.

to fight the good fight. If you're not careful, the outdoors will indeed kill you.

When I was a kid, many of my games with my friends involved a single rule: the ground was lava. If we were outside, then the grass was molten fire, and our only way to avoid rapid incineration was by hopping from lawn chair or swing set to Frisbee or rock. Indoors, the carpet was the sea of hellfire, and the bed was a boat.

This game might feel a lot like your life: suffering from the constant risk and paralyzing fear of drowning while your organs boil into soup. Now, the average asshole might try to encourage you to breathe or meditate, or tell you that feeling safe is a state of mind. But I know better. I know the dangers are real. And with that in mind, I'm going to help identify for you some safe harbors out there in the lava-filled moat that is the outside world.

First, I've got one word for you ... Starbucks. These ubiquitous cafés are filled with depressed people already. Your brothers and sisters in arms. You and they can truly camp out there. That's what Starbucks is for; the cafés were built for depressives. Where else can you not budge literally for hours and no one thinks it's strange?

A lot of recluses get away with appearing to be non-recluses, when really all they're doing is using Starbucks *as their home.*

The Starbucks near my parents' house is populated by a bizarre array of characters, including a guy who brings to the café a DVD player, a TV, and a tall stack of DVDs. You could be that guy. Why not bring a blanket, too? Settle in. Get comfy.

Even top professionals use Starbucks. You can identify them by the stench of office on their shirts. You may be turned off by this. It's understandable if these yuppies remind you of the terrible fluorescence of your former working life.

But keep in mind the professionals are the only thing, aside from the bean-and-harvest artwork, keeping Starbucks from becoming an aromatic homeless shelter. So try not to judge too harshly, for they are providing legitimacy.

There is also a sense of community that can be found at Starbucks, and what's perfect about it is that it's a very vague, distant kind of community, so you don't have to be bothered with real relationships.

If you show up every day and someone gets too chummy, you are well within your rights to pretend to stop recognizing them. Claim to have facial amnesia or short-term memory loss or an allergy to their preferred pastry.

My hometown Starbucks community includes a serial killer—a quiet white man with a wild stare—who provides me with a light adrenaline boost every time I see him, even when my system is producing nothing but sleep-inducing melatonin.

Don't be scared of the serial killers. Go out and explore your local Starbucks. You'll be comfortable among those people. No one is innocent there. That sweet old guy behind the counter is a mob hit man turned informant. And that well-dressed woman waiting behind you in line? She sells heroin to middle schoolers.

But once you've spent enough time at Starbucks and are starting to get bored (or burned out, like their coffee beans), you're ready for the next step in your community building. It's time to expand. Let's pay a visit to your closest local public library.

Libraries are one of the most important safe harbors for depressives, because antisocial behavior is the norm there. Everyone is expected to float around, silent and detached, like ghosts. There is usually ample seating. And like at Starbucks, a lot of homeless people roam the library, so in comparison you might actually look relatively put together.

A library is also a great place to pretend you're a genius. Stand in a really impressive area of the stacks, maybe the German literary criticism section. Flip back and forth, check the indexes, and try to look as harried as possible. Grunt a bit, then mumble: "This edition doesn't seem to offer the Lisbon translation. Typical!" The pretension will waft off your skin like oxidized garlic.

Then, when you're worn out from all the huffing and puffing, you'll need something to eat. May I suggest that you go to a lunch spot for an office you don't work at. What better way to be left alone than to hide among the working stiffs?

If you can find a sandwich counter in the lobby of some building or suburban office park, no one will bother you. Believe me, there's no group of people less friendly or likely to talk to you than disgruntled professionals in the middle of a workday.

There's also something nice about being right up close to the working people when you are still unemployed. It will remind you to be deeply thankful.

And my final piece of advice for creating safe spaces: get yourself an easel and canvas and stick them inside your car. This will give you permission to pull over in all sorts of odd places. All you need to do is take out your equipment and set it up next to your car, and, of course, people will assume you're an artist.

At that point, you can do whatever you want, even sleep. If anyone questions you, just say you're waiting for the right light.

Especially if you're pulled over at the side of a highway out in the countryside, you definitely don't have to worry too much about what people think. And the rural atmosphere is a great halfway house for the former home-depressive in general. The expectations for how you dress are certainly reduced.

I know when I'm out in the boonies and have to make a run to Rite Aid for some discounted Halloween candy and a tub of Tucks Medicated Cooling Pads, I'll throw on some high-waisted Nike relaxed-fit running pants and I'm good to go. It doesn't matter that the pants are my mom's and too small for me. (Aside: is it wrong to be larger than your mother?) People don't care about fashion in the country!

I round out the ensemble with a lightweight cotton mock turtleneck and some slip-on dress loafers. Then, as I head to Rite Aid, I think to myself: *Even if people did care about how I looked, who cares. I'm doing what I have to do to take care of my family, and that's what matters. Okay, I have no family and am not doing any caring except for my hemorrhoids, but no one else knows that.*

Truth be told, I don't change up my dress style even when I'm in New York City. I may add some eccentric flourish just to let everyone know I've heard of fashion, even if today is an "off day." Does that make sense? So basically it will be the same outfit as I wore out in the country, but I'll be taking an urban stroll to the Duane Reade for fish oil and chocolate-covered pretzels, and I'll add to my outfit a dramatic scarf or porkpie hat.

Another fashion-related tip as you venture into the outside world is to simply adopt a uniform—that is, something you wear every day. If you feel like it, go whole hog and pick up a charity T-shirt and clipboard. You'll have the added benefit of causing people to avoid you.

To be clear: you're going outside, and that's a great first step, but keep it in perspective. You're not going to be a fashionista around town, you're not going to be a social butterfly, and you're not going to radiate any joie de vivre. But with a few simple tricks, you can create the *appearance* of all of this.

. . . .

TOP EIGHT WAYS TO EXUDE ZEST FOR LIFE DESPITE LACKING A WILL TO LIVE

1. Carry an ice-cream cone covered with rainbow sprinkles. Eat it if you like; it doesn't matter. No one will notice. I myself always opt to actually eat the cone, and as a result I am not only perceived as jolly, but actually jolly in the way that Jolly Old Saint Nick is: overweight.

2. If you're concerned that weight gain will make you look sluggish, trust me, don't be. If you wear bright colors and sweatshirts emblazoned with cheerful sayings, you will be perceived as having a "large personality." And we're not out to fix society's fat-ism. We're just looking to get you down the street disguised as someone semi-cheerful.

3. Wear a red backpack. Not maroon. Not plum. True red. There's something about bright-red dyed canvas that lets the world know you have intentions to camp. Tuck a few granola bars in your pack and you might as well be saying, "Let's go, folks! Up and at 'em! Bright and early!"

4. If you're a man, wear flip-flops. Women can do it, too, but it's not as much of a statement. Also, flip-flops don't look weak in the way big slippers might, largely because of the "thong," the thing

that gnaws at the crotch of your big and second toe. That thing hurts, and thus it shows commitment to fun. You've gotta clutch that thong and press down with your toes a bit to keep the goddamn flop on your foot; there's more pain and work to a flip-flop than a person would suspect. That's why a flip-flop doesn't imply depression. It shows desire, commitment, and a likelihood that you might be off to the corner store to pick up some brewskies. It suggests you're willing to use toe strength so that you can feel the breeze on your feet. And "feeling the breeze on your feet" is a legendary hallmark of the life-loving sort.

5. Women, if you have longish hair, try a high ponytail. I always wear a cheerleaderly high pony. The ponytail counteracts the grimness of your otherwise expressionless face. It's like putting a bow on a rotting apple: certainly worth a try.

6. Wear sunglasses and sweats and carry a massive iced coffee. Pretend you have a terrible hangover because you "partied so much last night." A hangover is the perfect way to reframe your shuffling gate, puffy face, and incomprehensible mumbling. Most crowded parties consist of me "making my way" to the bar, the food, and then the door. Depending on how packed the venue, this can take twenty-five minutes.

7. Is "party" what people say these days? I don't

want to date myself, because I've fallen behind in the social scene for a few years. I don't want to be like my dad, who always refers to people enjoying a band or a piece of art as "getting off on it," without understanding that I immediately picture someone feverishly tugging his dick like he's shaking up cocktails.

8. Convince people that your silences signify something other than your depression. If someone comments on the fact that you don't say much, stay silent a moment longer, and then in a hushed confessional tone say: "I feel like if I start talking, I'll just be gushing." Or: "I'm trying to be a better listener, and you're very interesting." Or, the old standby: "Oh my God. I'm sorry. I was having a sexual fantasy and, yes, you were in it."

. . . .

CHAPTER TWENTY-TWO

....

BAD-WEATHER FRIENDS:
LET YOUR DEPRESSIVE ANTISOCIAL HABITS DESTROY THIN FRIENDSHIPS, REVEAL THE REAL TROUPERS, AND MAKE WAY FOR MORE DEPRESSOS

I learned way back in college, with Dawn, that whenever possible you should seek out friends who are as depressed or more so than you are—it will make you feel like a real ace. This same advice applies when you head back out into a world filled with other human beings after years holed up in your bedroom.

It is too much to expect you to have meaningful relationships with other creatures of the *Homo sapiens* variety right off the bat. At first you're going to see other people talking, and it will feel like they're speaking a different language. But with a little work, you can ease in and eventually bullshit with the best of them.

By bullshitting, I just mean appearing as if you're capable of carrying on conversations. When you're having one of these real, face-to-face interactions, people will often expect to hear what you "think." It's outrageous, when you consider what is actually being asked of you in these situations.

Not only are you supposed to hear and digest the content of their words but then work things over in your own head in front of these people, building on their thoughts, incorporating their comments into yours. It's messy work if done legitimately, which is why you should remember to bullshit.

You will be amazed at the stuff you can invent when you let go of trying so hard to think well. Don't think, just talk. If a friend seeks your opinion on why she continues to get into emotionally abusive relationships with Sound Designers named Todd, just open your mouth and go stream-of-consciousness on her for about thirty seconds. Then, just as abruptly, shut up and look wise.

Your friend will be forced to make meaning out of whatever convoluted bullshit you spewed her way. You'll be like a walking fortune cookie.

Some people will attempt to discredit your wisdom and accuse you of "pulling it out of your ass." What a laugh. In a world of common plagiarists who pluck the low-hanging fruits of ideas from the nearest Wikipedia article, someone who pulls an idea out of his ass should be held in high esteem, should he not?

If anyone accuses you of pulling an idea—say, about the long-term solution to our energy crisis—out of your ass, you should say thank you.

You may find it hard, at this point in your journey, to imagine yourself talking like that. You may find it a stretch to envision yourself having conversations at all. When you're depressed, obviously the idea of company is often disturbing. You haven't behaved like an actual person in weeks! You probably feel more blob than human. Being around people who have their shit together is an invitation to feel even worse.

But a properly depressed friend—someone who also wants to be alone and mope—can be delightful company. My friend Deirdre* is frequently depressed, and it's wonderful for me. I've found that when two depressives get together (by phone, Skype, et cetera, no pressure to go anywhere), they can have a shockingly good time.

When you're depressed, it's a vicious circle: you hate yourself because you're depressed and you're depressed because you hate yourself. But when you hang out with other depressed people, you can actually spend a few hours with humans without being completely bowled over by how much better they are than you.

There are so many fun things for two depressos to do, even remotely.

---

* I sent a text message to Deirdre, telling her I was happy to change her name in this book to protect her identity as a depresso. She texted me "no no no leave," followed by a second text saying, "LEAVE IT," and, finally, in explanation, "Trying to eliminate stigmas." Hooray for Deirdre!

· ·

TOP NINE THINGS FOR DEPRESSOS
TO DO TOGETHER

1. Trade Seamless.com logins. Set each other food order challenges—calamari that has NOT been fried beyond recognition but reveals itself as the rubber Thing it is, cheeseburgers from a Chinese restaurant.

2. Brainstorm ways you could live off the land together if you decide you can't make it in the real world.

3. Do bodily experiments in tandem. What do you feel when you press under and up your ribs with tensed fingers?

4. Practice telepathy together. Think of a word and have the other person guess it. Eventually you won't have to waste all that breath communicating.

5. Develop a modified language to use together that requires less vocal horsepower.

6. Agree to drop all gerund-related *g*'s. Say, *sleepin', cryin', dyin'*. Pull shortened, easier forms of words from a variety of dialects and accents. Pronounce the *th* sound as a simple *ta* or *da*. Don't finish off challenging vowel sounds. Instead of saying *why,* just say *wa,* or in place of *my,* just say *ma.* Drop the pronoun *I* entirely. It's never necessary. Your friend knows you're talk-

ing about yourself, again and always. When speaking in the past tense, give up use of the word *was* in favor of adding a *z* sound to the beginning of the next word. "I was walking around the apartment, thinking where are my meds" becomes far more digestible as "z'walkin' round da flat, tinkin' where ma meds."

7. When you pronounce words like *you* and *are*, picture that you're saying *u* and *r*. It's less tiring. Also, don't be fooled by the letter *W*. Never abbreviate a word with the letter *W*. It almost always takes longer to say. *World Wide Web* is only three syllables. *Double-yoo-double-yoo-double-yoo* is roughly sixty.

8. Compare the darkness behind your eyelids. Close your eyes and discuss what you see. Is it pure black? Brown? Floating lights? Does a devil man appear?

9. Compete to see who is more pathetic by forwarding e-mail evidence from your depressed lives, such as:

   a. E-mail to boss saying that despite today's unexplained absence, you promise you'll be in tomorrow, followed by e-mail to boss saying that again, you're not coming in.

   b. E-mail to an old flame that both requests sex and threatens suicide simultaneously.

   c. E-mail from old flame asking if you've gone
      off your meds.

   d. E-mail to old flame telling him/her you meant
      to send that e-mail to someone else.

   e. E-mail immediately following to old flame
      telling him/her that you lied, because you
      were ashamed and you still love him/her.

   f. E-mail immediately following that one to
      old flame challenging him/her to live in
      present and just marry you because you
      think it's a good idea and you're a known
      genius.

   g. E-mail from old flame asking about meds
      again, this time demanding answer.

• •

But you and your friend might want to agree to some depression ground rules first. Make it clear that neither of you is required to behave in any way resembling a constitutionally sound human being. And confirm that either party may cancel or bolt (by sluggish crawl) at any moment without feeling a need to explain why.

As you start to redevelop your social skills with your friend, slowly you'll practice the art of conversation. But there is one intermediate step . . . talking on the phone. This is something you can do when you're still under your covers in bed.

First things first: when I talk to someone on the

phone, I just picture immense blackness, and then I envision the person I'm talking to as a little being floating in that vast space. I, too, am floating, swaddled only by infinity. It's fairly horrifying.

A good trick is to wrap yourself up super tight in your blanket, so you feel all the more safe and hidden from the watchful eyes of the person you're talking to.

Or do something totally outrageous while on the phone with the other person. Make the call in the nude, while cooking. It will make you feel like you have all the power.

If you're worried you won't be able to think of anything to say to the person on the phone, keep in mind that in business, they say the person who talks the least in a negotiation has the most power.

Try it! One minute you'll be bare-assed, watching the microwave turn your Stouffer's Turkey Tetrazzini round and round, and the next you'll experience a dramatic shift of power between you and the L.L. Bean salesman on the other end of the phone.

But you must remember to remain silent, nothing more coming out of your mouth than a mumbled product number and your choice of Heather Gray. (Even though L.L. Bean has a website, it really ruins things to imagine them not shipping items out of a cabin.)

Once you've mastered the phone call, you're ready to move on to the next step of social interaction. The key is to be as you are. Forget about pleasing others. Forget about politeness. Enough will kick in naturally.

Our culture forces us to participate in these little social gestures. We're supposed to force a smile when a toddler rolls past in his carriage. I used to be a victim of this myself. I was afraid that if I saw your baby and didn't smile, you'd perceive it as me thinking the baby was ugly. Also, as a woman, I feared that if I didn't pretend to be charmed by babies I'd be hung as a witch.

Why was I the one feeling shameful or apologetic toward these mothers? What about all the times their little boy-child accompanied them into the women's restroom and stuck his head under the stall and looked at me? *While my pants were around my ankles.*

And then, to add insult to injury, when I come out of the stall and see the mom, *I'm* the one expected to smile. Like I was charmed by having a five-year-old peeking at my vagina.

It's too much, all the social responsibilities and etiquette we're supposed to perform in this country. It's up to us, the silent depressed masses, to stand up against this tyranny.

I haven't totally outgrown the fake niceties. Sometimes, when I'm not in a terrible mood and I've gotten a bit of Adderall-induced euphoria or just slammed an iced Americano, I'm bizarrely extroverted, even drawn to human interaction. It's almost like I bump into people on purpose so that I have to grin sweetly and say sorry.

At times like that, even those slack-jawed, bleary-eyed babies will get a wave and hello out of me, as though their dumb ogling deserves a response. But the five-year-old peering under the stall will get nothing from me. Nothing *ever*.

The point is, when you interact with other people, you should do what *you* want to do. Be the authentic depressive that you have become. You may be inclined to reach toward the "better" angels of your nature, the happy-go-lucky person beneath the depression. Fuck that. Be Hyde when you're Hyde. Jekyll can take responsibility for Jekyll.

Be genuine. If you're angry, be angry. Some people say depression is anger turned inward. So when you're a depressive heading out into the world, it can be helpful to try to turn your anger outward.

I've been doing this myself. Recently, I walked past a girl on the street who was on the phone and telling a friend she had to reschedule because she'd double-booked. I thought to myself, *Yeah, I seriously doubt that.* But instead of just thinking it, I said it to her ... like thirty feet after we passed each other, but still.

I rarely go all the way and yell at people, except in my sleep, which supports the idea that I have some buried anger. Almost nightly, in fact, you'll find me shouting at full volume, things like "This is fucking bullshit!" and "Shut the fuck up!"

I'm quite a menace.

But when I'm awake, even if my instinct is to stay quiet, these days I try to let it out, open the floodgates so that maybe the tide will dislodge some other buried anger from deep inside my emotional plumbing.

One day recently, I found myself suddenly angry toward my blender because the damn thing is so hard to clean. So what did I do? I didn't calm myself down. Instead, I threw the whole machine in the garbage. Then I started throwing all this other stuff in the garbage (atop the garbage, 'cause it's overfull)—all things I still use. My one can opener, which still has the most recent sawed-off lid attached, because "the fuck with my attempts at artichoke dip." Next a pan with burnt cheese I don't have a sponge capable of handling. Then a formidable steel sponge I come across, because I already threw out the pan it would have been used on . . . and you can't look backward in this life. All these novelty magnets because "they aren't strong enough to call themselves magnets but are weak . . . like me." The direction card to a wedding venue, because they should really put that info online, and I don't believe in monogamy.

I needed to feel my feelings. This kind of emotional flood happens so rarely, and passes so quickly, that I get a big rush from it. It makes me feel like a real person. I felt something, and I took action based on the feeling! It's what humans do.

That said, if you're gonna angrily trash possessions, you should probably choose stuff that's unsentimental—unless you're going for some serious emotional shock-and-awe. You may regret taking that baked-clay footprint art piece you made in nursery school and breaking it over your knee, screaming, "Her innocence is dead, her footprint is bullshit!"

Then again, maybe it's just what you need. Maybe you live in a ridiculous perfect shrine to your childhood, and you need to get a clue. In that case, smashing your porcelain bunnies could be quite meaningful and gorgeous, even cinematic.

Still, a good rule of thumb is to not smash anything with eyes. It's always sad later, when you're picking up the crushed beak of a parrot you painted and loved as a child, a parrot you had joyously splashed colors across before depression turned you into a violent line segment.

My mom loves to recall the time I was superdepressed and covered all my mirrors with sheets. I didn't smash them, but it was similarly intense. I had been having trouble leaving the house to go see my friends because I was paralyzed in front of my mirror, in tears, trying to get my hair into an orderly position.

Since my hair just wouldn't cooperate, I decided that instead of worrying about my reflection, I would simply give up on reflections in general. The whole scene looked a bit morbid to my family members, especially since the Jews cover mirrors with sheets during shivas, when someone has died.

But this is what it means to be genuine with yourself and others. It's accepting your depression and living with yourself where you are, not where you want to be.

It means knowing the limits of your ability to behave in the way that the rest of the world does. And it means dipping your toes into the social waters but being okay with dropping the ball on social obligations and canceling on friends.

When I was growing up, there was nothing better than when school was canceled for a snow day. It didn't just mean no school; it was bigger than that. Snow was the universe's way of saying, "Shhh, no more human activities, no cars, hush now, earth, settle down." Snow just kindly smothers the world at large, isolating everyone.

Even newscasters—those relentlessly cheerful and competent morning people—encourage you to stay indoors. No one thinks you're weird for doing so. A snow day for the depressed person is like Halloween for the vampire: she can hide in plain sight.

Deep down, everyone just wants a snow day. When you suddenly cancel on friends, you are doing them a favor. You are in effect giving them a snow day, even if they didn't realize they wanted one.

When I'm depressed, I find it impossible to attend most social events. It's not the *being there* I fear—there's usually booze and dim lighting. It's the getting there that kills me. I'll lie around and think about everything I need to do to get from my bed, now, at four p.m., to such-and-such event at six p.m. I'll picture trying to stand. I'll think about how I'll wear this week's favorite tee, even though it tugs across the love handles. I make peace with love handles, because they are American. Then I remember the tee has an undeniably hued barbecue sauce stain up near the neck, evidence of the cause of the love handles below. Maybe I could wear it anyway but crack a joke about it at the beginning of every conversation I have tonight.

I'll start thinking that if I want to make it on time, I better get a move on. And that's where it falls apart. There's something about "getting a move on" that I find utterly repellant.

I have disappointed people on many occasions. And you can, too.

Are you worried about disappointing people? Are you panicking because right now you should be getting ready for your friend's baby shower/clothes swap/Super Bowl party?

Let me put you at ease. Only a few people there will truly miss your presence, and depending on how erratically you've been behaving recently, they might be concerned you would only show up and be a downer anyway.

And if those people don't understand that "showing up" isn't securely in your wheelhouse, then you are bound to run into problems with them anyway. You need to acclimate these friends to your ways.

First, just blow off a few small events, like coffee and lunch dates. That way, when you *do* show up, you'll be greeted like a returning Ulysses. But for now, just cancel. Make an excuse. Nothing wrong with lying. Your friend doesn't want to hear the subtle reasons you are incapable of taking the subway two stops and letting her buy you a tuna sandwich. She'd much prefer to just hear you have a headache.

Better yet, use the migraine excuse. Migraines are a

pretty good approximation of the way your depression works, and no one can catch you in this lie. It is not uncommon for migraine sufferers to get one every few days.

Eventually, you might actually develop migraines through the power of suggestion, which you'll just love. The pain will be horrific, but you'll feel securely within your rights when you cancel on someone.

Also keep in mind that the first time you cancel on someone, you don't even really *need* an excuse. Regular people cancel all the time. Just say that you've double-booked, thusly suggesting you have more than one friend.

The second time you cancel on someone, acknowledge that you can't believe it's happening again. What a world! Apologize but imply fate and circumstance are at fault.

How you handle the third cancellation depends on your courage. If you feel the person has a wide sense of what's possible, you might opt to treat it as a sort of hat trick by the gods. In other words, you can count on the fact that in the normal world, someone having to cancel three times in a row is just so absurd that the person being canceled on can only assume it's by chance ... I mean, who would have the balls to cancel three times without a legitimate reason?

Even if you choose to blame fate for cancellation number three, you would be wise to heroically take on some of the responsibility—but only enough that the person thinks you are blaming yourself unnecessarily. Say something like "I am so deeply embarrassed and ashamed to say that I have to cancel yet again." Maybe then they'll encourage you not to beat yourself up.

Me, I have basically stopped making plans entirely. It just became too stressful to cancel all the time. It's very unnatural to tell someone that, no, you do not want to set a date next week, or next month, because you can't account for your mood, and in truth, you almost never actually want to go meet up somewhere.

In general, I just find it really strange that people are able to make a plan and then execute it at some later date. It feels as oppressive to me as a wedding betrothal at age three.

If you are this way, too, all I can recommend is that you find a lot of people who are like you and only want to socialize when it works out spontaneously. There are more than enough degenerates out there, other depressives and severe alcoholics, who will disappoint you often enough to warrant your doing the same to them. These are, in fact, some of my most cherished friendships.

. . . .

TOP FOUR EVENTS THAT ARE OKAY TO BAIL ON

1. Grandparents' funerals. If you miss, say, your best friend's funeral, your nonattendance will be

attributed to your grief. A grandparent's death, however, is almost a rite of passage, a moment we all can anticipate in our lifetimes. In other words, you should really be up for it, and your absence will come across as incredibly callous or make it seem as if he or she molested you. This makes a grandparent's funeral a *real* depressive's bail. I was late to my grandmother's funeral because I overslept and missed my flight home. I rushed and made it, but I ended up wearing a skintight thick, stretchy dance club top, which might have been worse than staying home. My former Girl Scout troop leader was there, and she no doubt regretted not having had us earn a badge on Deemphasizing Breasts at Funerals. When my grandfather died, on the other hand, my mother held a shiva in our home, and a local rabbi came over to officiate the prayers. I had trouble finding an outfit, and then refused to come downstairs. At least I had the cover of grief and its erratic expressions to obscure what was no doubt my usual neurotic bullshit and extreme vanity.

2. Siblings' graduations. It's just plain rude to flake on graduations, which is why you should do it with regularity. If your family is the type to take photos with the cap-and-gowned son or daughter, you will end up conspicuously absent in these piano-toppers for the rest of your life. Your

family will continue to forget why you're not in the picture as they remark on it over the years. Feel free to remind them that you missed the event because graduations reminded you of the fact that your own "Commencement" from high school was in fact not the beginning they tell you it is, but the ending of a time when people saw hope for your future.

3. Best friend's best friend funerals. If someone close to you loses someone close to him or her, someone whom you do not know, and you offer to support them by attending the funeral, you will probably find yourself incapable of doing so when that morning arrives. Look, the insistence on funerals being in the morning is rude to those of us who already find mornings demonic. A nice after-dinner-funeral, where you might show up drunk, would be a vast improvement, although it's true that mornings are so tough already that in some ways nothing feels *more* appropriate to the time of day than to attend a funeral. Especially on Mondays. Nothing is worse than getting stuck at a funeral with jerkels who don't want you to "mourn" their mother's death, but "celebrate" her life. Please. So now it's a cruise to Baja Mexico all of a sudden, but with no boat or Baja? I'm supposed to get up early *and* be happy about it?

4. Intimate gatherings thrown for a friend who is

moving. If you've been chosen as an invitee to a small gathering for only the closest of friends, the pressure will be so great that even if the event is being held in your own living room, you might find it impossible to attend. Trust that instinct.

• •

....

CHAPTER TWENTY-THREE

EXPLORE THE WHOLE "HAVING A BODY" THING AS A BREAK FROM THE PRISON OF YOUR MIND:
THE DEPRESSIVE ON FITNESS AND DIET

When you go out into the world after years at home, your body feels like a heavy corpse that you're trapped inside. There was probably a time long ago when you and your body were in a semi-cooperative relationship. But that was then. Now you're going to have to develop a new working relationship with this skin-suit of yours. It's a process that requires delicacy, like a man with his newly amnesiac wife.

The first step to reconnect with your body is to breathe into its lungs. This one is still a tough pill for me to swallow, but people who get in the habit of breathing regularly report great things. Since it only takes a few minutes without oxygen to straight-up die, it seems reasonable that even a small increase in the amount of air you consume might make you feel vaguely less dead.

Now don't be a hero and try for the long, deep breath. Experiencing that "good God, I'm alive" feeling so suddenly might cause you to recoil like a vampire from the light. At first just try a wee puff, as from a questionable doobie.

Besides breathing, you'll want to start cleaning your body really carefully. If you can make it to the bathroom, give yourself a full detailing. Who knows how long it will be until the next time you're motivated enough to bathe? So instead of doing the bare minimum in there, like you usually do, this time do the maximum. Employ sea salts. Baking soda. Perhaps something utilizing the proverbial turkey baster? Dry yourself with a boat chamois—a tiny, stiff, profoundly absorbent little square that is much lighter than a terry-cloth towel. There are ways to substitute efforts you find exhausting with ones you find more manageable. I found lathering shampoo to be a bit too much on the ole triceps, so I'd premix shampoo with water in a big bottle, shake it, and apply prelathered.

Then, once your body is clean, it's time to use it. I'm not going to actually suggest walking, running, dancing, aerobics, yoga ... as though you've never heard of the benefits of doing such activities for thirty to sixty minutes. That works for functioning people who have "things to do," and so their workouts must be quick and effective.

You, on the other hand, have nothing to do, so your

workouts should be drawn out and semi-ineffective and should kill as much time as possible. Try strengthening one muscle group at a time. Tense one of your butt muscles until you're exhausted.

Or do constant Kegels. In mere weeks you will be the Schwarzenegger of Pubococcygeus. When you "get out" of depression you'll have either (a) a vagina like a vise or (b) a penis with a hands-free wiggle capacity angle increase of 10 to 50 percent—depending on your current abilities.

Anything that works up a sweat is good. Even if it means sitting in front of a space heater until you drip. While you haven't exercised, it might trigger some positive memories associated with it. Eating a big meal after a good sweat of any sort feels wonderful. That's why the Russians eat smoked fish in the sauna. I've done a lot of unfunded research on pigging out in general and can help you through the tricky parts.

First of all, don't try to beat the system by finding ways to scarf without consuming too many calories. Know you're going to eat the entirety of anything you buy. So if you insist on looking at the nutritional information, just do a quick multiplication of calories per serving by servings per container to know what you'll be ingesting. Discard the farce that is the "chip clip."

Then, after you make peace with the total quantity of cals, assess how long the food will take to eat if you move at an athletic pace. Before purchasing anything, you need to know how long the item can keep you in that suspended state of grace known as "being in the middle of eating."

Account for start-up and wind-down times when you choose a snack.

For the first few minutes of eating a food, you'll barely feel settled into the idea that you're eating it, and so a portion needs to allow for a good minute or two of eating before you even make a dent. Otherwise, it'll be over before it starts.

Don't ever dismiss the importance of size or quantity when it comes to food. Sometimes you hear people talk about relishing a small but rich and luxuriant piece of chocolate cake. They say it's all about savoring those few sumptuous bites, then setting down the fork, and feeling like some kind of woman.

Not for us.

We must go for large quantities of almost every food, enough to move through our body and an entire evening like a slow-moving storm system. What we're looking for is that nice sense of abdominal heaviness, in which you can relax and maybe be put to sleep. There's something about abdominal bloat that just pulls you out of your head and into your gut like nothing else.

Some depressives try to change their lives by adopting a new regimen of healthy eating. My recommendation? Don't.

For a while I thought I could really beat the system when I started making pasta dishes using shredded coleslaw veggies in place of noodles. Throw that slaw into boiling water for a minute and strain! It's quite effective when you're really just there for the sauce and Parmesan.

But one night as I was contemplating making a pizza without dough, I found my way into the artisan section of the market. It's near the cold cuts, and it offers a lot of cheeses and olives and fresh bread and pasta.

It was there that I had a profound realization based on an age-old stereotype: in Italy there are large men who love nothing more than Momma's meatballs and don't sweat it.

Not just in Italy. If we're to believe what we see on TV, there are guys everywhere with huge bellies of fat crowding out their organs, men who are probably not going to live exceptionally long, sure—but they're happy, and they eat to feed their souls.

Yes, in "feeding their souls," they eventually cause said souls to eject out of their bodies from heart disease, but then at least they become fat-but-happy ghosts who haunt the kitchen.

Anyway, it occurred to me that these men don't think of their eating as a horrifying habit, coping mechanism, or something to master or game. They just do it. And if they can be free of that shame, why can't I? For some reason I never realized this was an option.

I bet if I had an Italian uncle or something, he'd laugh at the idea of my "depression" and say, "Dontcha know? You're a Boyardee! You just haven't had my manicotti in a while. This is all is wrong."

Well, let me be your Uncle Boyardee and say that if you're going to use food to cope, you should do it with the spirit of a gourmet and get exactly what your heart of hearts—not the one with the arteries, but the mystical heart—craves.

Food is the coping mechanism of giants ... don't forget it.

I recently went through a phase in which I started to question this. I had become conscious of my gut and began to believe that all my problems stemmed from there. I suppose it was based on the never-ending Italian meals I cooked up. The Boyardee theory coming home to roost.

Supposedly, women shouldn't carry their weight in their guts like men. It's referred to as apple shaped, and it's considered the least healthy distribution of fat. It's not the glory of womanly curves seen in ass or thigh meat, but the organ-crowding gut you see pressing on the dress shirt of a 1950s businessman and heart attack victim. It's round and pressurized, and people have asked me more than once whether I am pregnant.

So I started researching the Master Cleanse. That's the "lemonade diet." I bought the tiny pamphlet in a health food store and decided it was to be my salvation. For a minimum of eight days, you eat nothing but lemonade made of water, lemon juice, maple syrup, and cayenne pepper.

You also drink laxative tea. You get your calories

from the maple syrup. After your body clears out your colon, it takes a break from digestion and goes to work on fixing your scar tissues and fear of flying. There are endless forums and blogs of people describing their Master Cleanse experiences, and so I did it and looked to them for support.

The best part of the Master Cleanse is the Salt Water Flush. You drink two big bottles of warm water that you've supersaturated with salt. Your body can't absorb all the sodium, and so it goes straight through you—if you can keep it down.

I realized one evening that I was unable to keep it down, and I ran to the bathroom. But before I had a chance to aim at the toilet, two huge bottles' worth of salt water came out of my mouth like a fire hose.

It's really amazing how the insides are able to project stuff so far out of the body. I mean, how does it do it? It's not like throwing liquid is easy even if you use your hands. Where does the pressure come from?

It was an interesting week. I had, as promised, gotten quite "clear." I'd taken apart my bed and purchased a small foldout sofa bed from IKEA, in hopes that I could live more like a little soldier.

I lost weight and became incredibly focused. I'd join my parents for dinner, and, as they ate a regular meal, I'd juice my lemons and speak to them with the giddy mania of a fasting zealot.

On the eighth day, I traveled from my parents' house to western New York to perform stand-up comedy* at a one-nighter charity event. Before I went onstage, nerves caused me to forget I was on the cleanse, and so I ordered a White Russian from the bar.

Actually, what happened was I saw someone drinking something creamy and frothy and thought, *Now that looks like a good drink,* probably because it most resembled food. After I performed, and realized I had broken the cleanse, I took my check and drove straight to a strip mall near the Comfort Inn where I was staying.

There was one Chinese restaurant open late. I tried to order something gentle. The pamphlet recommends you break the cleanse by "eating" only orange juice for a day and then vegetable broth for a few days after that. Those ease-off days are not even included in the fasting days. What a joke. I adjusted the suggestion and ordered a vegetable soup, a Buddha's Delight, and a side of brown sauce and brown rice.

I took it all back to the Comfort Inn with an excited feeling deep in my stomach that was so profound I couldn't have described it at the time if I had tried; it turns out it was hunger, but I'd forgotten the word.

I was aware of what a profound meal this would be. Because of my days of fasting, I was also more capable of restraint than usual, so I didn't race to my room

---

* Yes, I've been withholding mentions of my stand-up comedy throughout this book, because no one likes a comedian. That being said, check out my album, *Quality Notions,* on iTunes.

but spent twenty-five minutes choosing a DVD from a binder at the front desk. I decided on *300*, the movie about Spartans. I took the DVD and the large, heavy brown paper bag to my room.

I removed the semenous top quilt and blanket, settled myself on the fresh sheets of the bed, and opened the takeout bag. The satisfaction of pulling apart the paper was erotic, but without the sin and guilt of sex. As the staples popped off, it was like meeting God and deserving to.

I realized then that they hadn't included any utensils. So I was forced to eat the soup with my hands, which was magnificent, pouring the liquid into my mouth and dipping fingers into the plastic pint to clutch the vegetables. I enjoyed the movie a great deal, rated it a "delicious and satisfying film," and went to sleep very happy.

The next morning I drove home and stopped at a variety of rest stops, enjoying a chicken sandwich at Burger King and a frosted doughnut from Dunkin' Donuts. It was magical.

I went back to my old ways for some time, still hoping that the cleanse had healed me somehow. Hey, you never know what straw will break the depression camel's back. I did end up moving out of my parents' house only a few weeks later, so maybe the cleanse did something for me. Or maybe it was the soldier's cot.

I didn't try another digestive overhaul like that until just recently. I wasn't up for all that lemon squeezing again. So instead I started researching recreational colonics, also called hydrotherapy.

Someone puts a hose in your rectum and shoots water up your colon until you are simply dying for a release. Then they flip a switch, allowing you to drain everything out through the hose, carrying the feces of yesteryear into the city's plumbing.

Of course, this sort of inner detailing was immensely appealing to me. Rumor has it that people sometimes expel crayons and pennies they swallowed as children. The idea is that if you remove the gunk lining your GI tract, it will digest nutrients better and shoo along waste more efficiently, and this will improve your mood.

Now there are certain things you want to buy retail, and for me, an anal hosing just wasn't one. I found a threefer on the Lifebooker website and made an appointment with someone in my neighborhood in Manhattan. She had two offices, one in a facility and one in her private home. Since the facility was a subway ride away, I opted to go to her in-home ass-blast studio, which I could easily walk to, and, I imagined, hobble home from on foot, sore but shining.

When I got to her building, her husband let me in. He was very friendly and plump. His wife, the therapist, was Chinese and had an accent that caused me to occasionally nod even when I didn't understand what she was telling me.

She showed me into a tiny bathroom in a hallway, right next to the kitchen where her husband was cooking in his socks, sautéing bok choy for their dinner. I told her I was there because my stomach looked pregnant, and she said, "I know, I can see!" Her comment stung a bit, but at least I was in the right place.

The bathroom had been redesigned for exclusive colonic use. The sink was rigged to some kind of little machine that managed the entrance and exit of fecal waters. In the bathtub stood a cheap folding bar table, which she instructed me to mount. I struck the fetal position. She ripped open the plastic packaging of a fresh hose and attached it to the machine, and then prepared me for the insertion.

I asked if I could quickly grab my phone from my purse, as I knew I'd want to text pictures of my face to my friends during the procedure. She obliged; this seemed to be a common request. When I felt the cool whistle-like end of the tube grazing my pinched entrance, she started telling me to "push."

So I began pulsing my asshole at her, but she continued to bark at me to "Push!" It must have looked like a little flower trying to bloom, and she, being an expert, spotted my exertion. I know she did, because in her thick accent, she cried out, "No, push it in! Push it in!" and then she took my hand and placed it on the hose.

I had cockily assumed that when she told me to push, she was using commoner's language for *bear down,* thinking I wouldn't know the appropriate term. But in fact she wanted me to take the hose, insert the whistle myself, and push it in—and all the response she was getting was my flexing my ass at her like a mute frog trying to croak.

A frog with a frog in its throat.

She was very nice about it afterward.

And my stomach *was* flatter for a while, but like a Tempur-Pedic mattress, it soon returned to its original shape.

My latest fantasy of reducing my abdominal distension without giving up scones is that I have some kind of noncancerous mass in the lower abdomen bulking things up. My cousin had one removed that was the size of a grapefruit, which (in case you are unfamiliar with fruit) is approximately the size of a D-cup breast. Once removed, I'd still have a belly-fat blanket, but it would lie flatter. I'd surely be more inspired to get rid of it. For now, I feel it's best to hold off on improving my diet until I've had a transvaginal ultrasound. This time, when the OB/GYN tech tells me to "push," I'll know to grab the wand myself.

I read once that if you try to talk to your ailment or even your excess fat and kindly ask it why it's there, it will give you an answer. For example, you might ask a wart and it might tell you that it wants you to make room for ugliness in your life. In that scenario, you would then start allowing your child's hideous clay art to live on your Noguchi coffee table, and the wart could go away.

It's all about talking to the *soul* of the ailment or issue. That way, the answers that come back to you will be mystical, not annoyingly practical. The soul of a belly roll isn't going to growl back at you, "It's the mozzies! It was the mozzarella sticks the whole time!"

I once attempted this strategy and asked my belly why it insists on storing my weight in its area. It responded that it thought people would like me more if I had belly fat. I would never come off as a threatening bitch, just slightly incompetent, but endearingly so.

My belly also "said" that I had a potbelly as a child, and so belly fat would make me feel youthful. I felt like my belly was lying, but I turned a blind eye.

My focus on belly fat was a bit silly, but because depression so often reduces everything to meaninglessness, a vain and physical preoccupation can be a great way to stay grounded.

I was preoccupied, for example, with my hemorrhoids for many years. They were a highlight of my depression. An SSRI I was taking was making me very constipated, but in my eagerness to keep a blockage from happening, I would rally some ancient warrior spirits to come to my aid and really make it rain on that toilet.

I developed a strategy. I would adjust myself on the toilet so that each ass cheek had as wide a grip on its side of the seat as possible—so that my anus wasn't hidden deep in a crack of two cheeks, but fully exposed, and reaching toward the toilet water with all its might.

You know when butchers do that butterfly thing with meat? Where they slice it, open it like a book, and then pound it down? That's the effect I was trying to have on my butt.

No. It's more like my ass was a brand-new book, and my bowel movement was a bookmark deep inside the book. I was trying to open the book wide and soften the spine, to let the bookmark fall out on its own.

No war is won without casualties and bloodshed, but without hemms, I would never have known I had a warrior within.

Some people think you have to be athletic and physically impressive to be a warrior. Not at all: you just need to have a heroic sphincter. You can even become a warrior, a perfect human specimen, without moving. Forget running, forget lifting weights, forget moving at all, except from bathroom to bedroom. It's all mental.

I am not yanking your chain. If you think bulging muscles are what stand between you and joy, all you need is to begin a mental regimen of *imagining* you're doing bench presses.

You've probably read the articles, but I'll remind you of everyone's favorite study's conclusion: if you envision doing something, your mind actually believes you're doing it.

If your mind believes you're using your muscles, it probably tells the endocrine system to act as if it is, at which point I'll bet it releases certain chemicals—basically steroids and a metabolism booster. I'm confident it's like taking a heavy combination of invisible 'roids and methamphetamines, just like a baseball player in the '90s, except untraceable.

The only problem is that mentally going through

the experience of crunches can be almost as uncomfortable as doing them. But keep your eyes on the prize. The exercise routines of the depressive are grueling, but they are worth it. Your body is your temple, and your trash can.

···

CHAPTER TWENTY-FOUR

LET'S DO IT, LET'S FALL IN LOVE:
RUN INTO THE OCEAN OF LOVE WITH YOUR DEPRESSION SHOES STILL ON

It has become a cliché in therapy that you can't love another until you love yourself. I would ask you to put aside that oft-repeated claim and hear me out. True, at first it might not seem wise to get involved with other people while you aren't firing on all cylinders. Maybe you are still filled with a general sense of shame and self-hatred. Or maybe it's the rituals of dating themselves. Why eat ice cream while someone wins you a stuffed frog when you could be in your car with the windows up, charting your emotions under a new therapeutic rubric?

But things have changed, now that so many more people are depressed. Men and women with all sorts of problems are getting out there, and you should, too. Don't hold back. It's like a school where all the kids are coming in sick. Why should you stay home if they aren't?

And, in fact, being a depressive gives you unique skills and opportunities in the arenas of love and sex, assets that aren't available to the nondepressed. For example, one great thing about being depressed is that you can really date anybody, since your standards have fallen away, along with other assessment abilities.

Being depressed also gives you a certain appeal in the romantic and sexual marketplace. Don't sell yourself short. There's a lot that your disease brings to the table. Think of it this way: you know how in relationships you often hear about people's personalities clashing? That is: "He was such a control freak, and I like to live in the moment." Or the opposite: "He never has a plan, and I'm just not that spontaneous."

Well, good news. Because of your decreased energy, all of your qualities are probably muted. Your personality is softer around the edges. You will not clash with your partner, because you're just not strong enough. If personalities are colors, your color right now is so diluted it's practically white. And white goes with everything.

And if there are things about your partner's personality that bother you, you still probably won't have the energy to bristle or complain. All the attitudes that normally jeopardize relationships are totally out of your capacity at the moment.

· ·

TOP FIVE ANNOYING THINGS PEOPLE DO IN RELATIONSHIPS THAT YOU WILL NEVER DO

1. Eye rolling. No way. It's hugely exhausting and largely for show. Eyes are for reading this book and shutting.

2. Attempting to control or change a partner. That's a laugh. You are so deep in the shit show of your own self that changing your partner isn't even on the horizon.

3. Denying sex. While you may not be excited by the sex, it is a great opportunity to get credit for doing something while still remaining in bed. Also, sex allows you the opportunity to play out unusual action-film scenarios in which you barely move, like the classic where you pretend to have been injected between the toes with a numbing serum. Can you achieve orgasm with the romantic lead before the effects reach the waist?

4. Expectations. You likely have none of those, as you have long ago abandoned any expectations of yourself. Actually, because you probably can't believe anyone could find value in your company, it might be useful to manufacture some expectations even if they're not coming naturally to you. Try saying, "I need a man who

will take complete responsibility for my daily water intake."

5. Demanding. When you say you don't care whether you eat Chinese or Mexican, you mean it. At first your partner will get angry with you for being passive aggressive. After a few experiences, he/she will learn you truly don't know what you want. A great restaurant is really no better than a shitty restaurant, because when everything's pointless and dissatisfying, one thing is really no better than another. So in that sense, you're "easy to please."

· ·

So don't be afraid to slouch toward romance. Fall in love if you want. Go wild. Have mad crushes and torrid affairs. Here are a few options you should consider when you're a depressive looking for a romantic partner:

Rich old guys. Given your willingness to nap through the afternoons, you can easily win the devotion of a geriatric Roosevelt or Astor. I've never dated a geezer, but I've heard great things about the experience, and I see it on TV all the time. Usually, the women who date men in their eighties and nineties are portrayed as bimbos, but you don't have to follow suit.

I suspect old men are not even necessarily that desperate for sex. Can they provide an erect penile offering? Unlikely. Most of them just want to keep the company of someone young, a person with a twinkle in her eye and a skip in her step.

Luckily for you, you don't need an actual twinkle or spring to communicate youth. Even at your most depressed you have a comparatively youthful glow. You can't help it. You may not see it, either. If you're under the age of eighty-five, you're likely blinded by your own youth.

But the eighty-five-year-old can see it. He knows what to look for. The way your wrist doesn't crack every time you wave. The way your face still rests more or less atop your skull and hasn't slipped down to hang around your neck like statement jewelry.

These are the things that scream vibrancy to your geriatric lover.

Also, your old man doesn't need to be that rich. If he has a place to live and enough cash to cover some groceries, that's rich enough for you. If you're unable to get a job or even buy groceries, anyone covering the basics should be deemed "rich."

Bonus: the elderly aren't as familiar with mental health issues. They're from the bootstrap days, and so talking to them about your depression won't really register. This can provide you some relief, because you don't have to talk about it all the time, and even if you do, you won't be understood. It forces you to discuss other things you don't normally talk about, like the price of canned peaches or discontinued hard candy, which can be a nice change of pace.

But keep in mind, just because you're depressed doesn't mean an old guy is your only option. This might seem crazy, but you shouldn't preemptively dismiss the possibility of dating somebody "normal," someone who is seriously alive and out making things happen. You know those people you hear about? The ones who are off-the-charts legit. Who suffer from chronic sleep deprivation because they're always "working" at a "job" where they "stay late" (sorry, I just love using their strange jargon).

I only know a few of these people personally, but I think they're the ones for whom scientists invented those small plastic containers of soup you can microwave in the office kitchen. I really don't know—I'm getting most of this information from movies, specifically the beginnings of romantic comedies in which the protag is a corporate animal, is always missing his/her kids' soccer games and recitals, and must learn over the course of the movie what truly matters in life: Jennifer Aniston.

But the person you date doesn't have to be legit only in traditional business either. Your significant other could be a run-of-the-mill rock star, constantly traveling the globe and up late at night scrutinizing his latest performance on the Video Music Awards.

Regardless, you know the type. The basic criterion these people meet is that they make daily efforts to further their goals and better themselves. They are not on pause. They are never on pause.

Your natural inclination is to avoid such people, for good reason. You're bound to compare your current situation to their productive lifestyles and fall into a deep shame spiral that gets a little extra spin every time your eyes fall upon their faces.

Also, their life includes dinners and events at which your attendance could be mandatory.

Basically, it's a nightmare. It's the antithesis to your way of life.

And for that reason, it just might provide you an awesome out, an ejector seat, should you ever decide to quit the lifestyle all together.

Sometimes baby steps are harder than gigantic, spastic leaps. Baby steps require a kind of self-acceptance in which you make peace with your progress no matter how humble, and you don't worry about how long it will take you to get where you want to go . . . and all that other bullshit.

It might be easier to do something totally absurdly out of your range—like dress up in black tie and take multiple subways to a fund-raising gala with a group of people you find repugnant—than it is to, say, walk to a FedEx and send in that W-9 form.

People who are off-the-charts legit can force you into situations you would never have the strength to arrange for yourself. They might, for example, decide to cook salmon at their home one night, and there you are, eating salmon like a person, sitting up at the kitchen table.

If this just sounds like too much of a stretch, you could always revert to your self-defeating ways and go for someone who obviously will never love you.

I know, the latter sounds emotionally dangerous. But I would instead think of it as a training exercise for the soul. It's a great way to develop your self-esteem—your true self-esteem, not the flimsy construct you build out of a lover's compliments and worshipful gazes.

Many people become dependent on a partner's affection, and the muscles of true self-esteem atrophy. It's just so much easier to eat up esteem that comes from outside of you. Generating self-esteem from within? It feels like a desperate, short-term solution, your body cannibalizing your muscles before you die of starvation.

If you can learn to love yourself while in a relationship with someone who does not love you, then you've done some very important work. You won't exactly be happy, but happiness is not in the picture right now anyway.

I dated a guy for a year and a half who ultimately revealed that he didn't love me. I mean, he didn't hate me and he definitely cared for me, found me amusing and worthy of sex, but he was not in love with me.

During that relationship, we enjoyed each other's company, went to dinner every night, and hit golf balls at a driving range. He often looked at me with something resembling warmth. I felt pretty good about myself at the time regardless, because I was doing that necessary "personal work," including some absurd yoga practices, i.e., a DVD called *Dance the Chakras*,* lots of meditation, and daily trips to Target. When he ended it with me, telling me he didn't love me, I was stunned in the moment, cried for a few days, and then moved on. No harm done.

Romantic relationships are a total shit show in regard to self-esteem, and when you tether your sense of self and mood to the responses of a crush, lover, or partner, you are in for a wild ride. It can be exciting, and you can justify it in a way you can't with other drugs. You can tuck all of your obsessive and unhealthy behaviors under the umbrella of love.

So there you are, thinking that "All You Need is Love" means you should send someone a text offering sexual favors, despite the other person's request that you only be friends. You think that "Love Will Conquer All" means that you should send a second text explaining that you were referring to a blow job and that it comes with no expectations of anything more than friendship. Secretly, you believe that once you have this person's genitals in your mouth, you can probably convince him to marry you.

---

* This incredible DVD employs facets of kundalini yoga to awaken the serpent of energy that lies curled sleeping at the base of your spine. Mostly through a lot of sensual movement and "ecstatic dance." When my father would step out from his office to refill his coffee, he'd hear me barking mantras as I swooped and gyrated, throwing invisible rose petals from my heart.

Once you've given a "marry me" blow job and had the person decide not to marry you, you are faced with managing your self-esteem with an urgency that an e-mail forward of Maya Angelou's "Phenomenal Woman" just won't provide you.

Unless your "marry me" blow job is just that good, in which case, well, congratulations on your upcoming nuptials.

Speaking of blow jobs, one of the main benefits of being generally diminished in spirit is that a lot of your sexual hang-ups will fly south for the winter. That fluttering nervousness you used to feel while stripping down to your bare essentials? Nothing more than a slight twitch now.

It's not that your depression has made you fearless. You're still paralyzed by having to make a phone call or attend an event with friends. No, it's that your fear is no longer so *diversified*. All its energy has become centralized, fixated on the big, impossible stuff: talking to people, maintaining an upright posture, switching your TV input from HDMI 1 to HDMI 2.

With all that to worry about, I have found there simply isn't enough anxiety left over for old worries like: when I strip down for sex, will my stomach look fat?

But let's talk about you. If you're out of the house, rubbing up on dudes in bars, you're obviously already doing pretty well in this area. You've overcome the scariest obstacles: you've put on clothes and headed out to socialize despite being an alien from a dull and haunted planet.

But there's still the draining prospect ahead of having to haul ass home with some Danny in tow. And if you focus on that challenge, you just won't have the energy to worry that your vagina looks like a tattered flag.

Depression can selectively free you of the fear of being judged. In *all* arenas, definitely sex but also just regular interactions. When I lose my debit card in my apartment, I just walk to the corner Chase and say I need help. I tell it to everyone in the bank in my remote vicinity, anyone who will listen. I don't try to handle it in a swift or even efficient manner or wait at the teller line. It's not my job to know how to work within *their* system.

I just take a seat in one of the young male associate's cubicles, have a lollipop, and tell them what's up.* I don't waste energy fibbing. I don't tell them my card is lost. I tell them the truth—it's probably in my apartment. In fact, I had it fifteen minutes ago when I used it to order a second copy of *Why Do I Think I Am Nothing Without a Man?* The associate is bound to fall for you. And you didn't even have to go to a bar!

That's another thing. When you start playing the flirting game as a depressive, you realize how little work it takes. Forget going to a bar. You can seduce 'em while barely moving. Which is perfect for you.

---

* I actually don't eat the lollipops, because banks offer the cheapest possible lollipops, the flat ones in square plastic wrappers.

Before long, you will see that you can live as much of a corset ripper of a life as the more outgoing, active set. I should warn you, however, that thanks to depression's dulling of the nerves, unsheathing of a man's vile tool won't provide the thrill it once did, though this detached perspective allows for a more academic reflection on the concept of male peninsular flesh while you dutifully fulfill its yearning demands.

Penises aside, one last warning I have for you is that depression can worsen sexual jealousy. When your self-esteem is in the red, you might begin to fixate on your lover's ex-lovers or your ex-lover's new lovers.

I almost never take the step of looking up these women on Facebook or Google, and I don't recommend that you do either. Then again, maybe doing that would make Her seem more real, so you stop elevating her to the level of a demigod.

But the greater risk is that it goes the other way. You could scroll for six seconds on the girl's Instagram feed and pick up a lifetime's worth of proof about why others are more suited for human existence or pulling off blunt bangs than you are.

Generally, I prefer to take the few minor details I've heard (or imagined) about the Other Woman and blow them up into mythic proportions in my mind.

The Other Woman is always everything I'm not. But even if she is something I am, she is always far better at it than I am. If I'm a mess, she's put together. If I'm a mess, and she's a mess, she's a beautiful mess.

The Other Woman is such a potent source of pain that your only real option is to use its power for fun.

While it's nice to hear a boyfriend whisper during sex that he's so attracted to you, you might on occasion request that he instead tell you how repulsive other women are, or how insipid or bad at Scrabble his ex-girlfriend was ... and how she was bad at Scrabble not in a cute way, but in a rude way. How she'd make up a word and then humorlessly defend its existence, and save you no guacamole if you challenged her.

No, the greatest gift a partner could give to his depressed, jealous gal would be to mime the stifling of a dry heave any time she drops the name of a shared female acquaintance.

CHAPTER TWENTY-FIVE

....

GET SERIOUS ABOUT YOUR HEALING:
BUT DON'T ACTUALLY HEAL UNTIL YOU'RE IN THE MOOD

Well, you finally made it to the last chapter in the book. Which could only mean that . . . could it really be true . . . are you starting to come out of the fog? This is tricky territory. Even if you are feeling better, maybe you don't want to start telling people yet? Keeping up the appearance of a depression for as long as possible is a great way to keep off your back all those dildos, also known as your friends and loved ones.

Another thing to watch out for: don't assume you're better and go off your meds. Let's say you've been on meds for a while now. At first you thought they were helping. Friends told you that you seemed better. But now you're feeling crappy and wonder whether the pills are still working.

I've been in this situation many times. The train of thought goes like this . . .

1. I've been on meds for a while now.
2. But I feel crappy.
3. The meds must not be working.
4. I'm certainly not in the mood to deal with calling about refills.
5. You know, the meds are probably the whole problem anyway.
6. Was I even depressed before the meds? Don't much recall.
7. I should go off them, like, right now.
8. Better call the psych.
9. But if I tell the psych, she'll say we should create a plan for easing off them to avoid dramatic mood changes. She might even try to dissuade me from going off the meds in general, but that's surely Big Pharma talking.
10. I think I'll just go cold turkey and see what happens.

Then, a few hours or days later, I start to feel strange. Perhaps a little hyper? A touch of hypomania, a wise friend asks? Hard to say! Who cares?

I start to list off to my friend Deirdre all of the reasons I can't wait to be fully done with meds forever. I'll be talking fast, using a lot of verbal outlining, and my mouth is dry, because I certainly did not go off the Adderall. That would be absurd.

So I continue my rant about meds. I list off Lexapro's side effects, and Deirdre agrees to listen.

I bring up the need for Ex-Lax and how the meds make you get hemorrhoids that blow up like in an action movie . . . seriously, it's like there's a special-effects monster lighting your ass on fire, and all you can do is bribe him to stay away with frequent gifts of fiber.

What am I talking about? Apparently, I'm rhyming now (*fire/fiber*). Deirdre doesn't acknowledge that, which is kind. But I can't help myself . . .

> Garden State *was right: meds mute the many colors*
> *of living,*
> *So I cold turkey'd it and stood with goose pimples*
> *shivering.*

I'm fully singing now. God, being off meds is great for unleashing creativity . . .

> *I can see! The world's beau-ty! A yellow bee! An*
> *emerald tree!*
> *Ooh! A many-hued worthless loser, wait, that's me.*

Okay, so some of the insights are a little negative, but they have energy, no? I continue:

> *My clarity's back. I can see . . .*

Hmmm. I'm coming up dry. A false start. Freestyling is hard.

> *My clarity's back. I can see . . .*
> *. . . that I've got nothing to give!*

Wait, what?

. . . but yeah, it's totally worth the joy of all this
    ROYGBIV!
Excuse me while I relish the yellowish hues
    of the threads in the rope with which I wind my noose!

Oh crap, this is getting a little dark, but still impressively worded, no? I really don't want to stop singing, which I'm certain will happen if I go back on meds, but my triumphant ditty about how great it is to be med-free is starting to contradict itself.

Meds just flatten you out, girl, like they told you
    before!
Though how much more flat can I get if this day's day
    four on this floor . . .

Hmmm. I realize how many med-free days I've spent on the floor recently. Also, this is becoming more of a rap, with an obnoxious, affected hip-hop style I don't deserve to use. I start to wonder whether those side effects were really worse than the depression, but still I refuse to stop singing. I decide finally that I better do a thorough review of the side effects and weigh the benefits. (Thanks again, Adderall!)

So A to D were G.I. BS, E—night sweats, F—dry
    mouth,
vision disturbance—G, H—dizziness, and I—nausea
    bouts,
but the occasional rash of feeling okay and getting out of
    bed

plus the flare-ups of a will to live do seem to form the
    rest of the alphabet.

Another side effect that hits girls, too, but different is
    impotence.
Dude's moby dicks do tend to get beached
in the less than inclement climate of your intimates.
But that's no hindrance if the glide's applied inches by
    increments.

And another pro of your labia minora——the majority
    being dry——
is on the nearby majora, pubic hair's got no fly-
aways, because no humidity makes it hardily pubicky
    hair
so there's no thirteen-dollar Frizz-Ease on your
    CVS ExtraCare . . . card.

Yeah, now that I've weighed everything, I am sure
that I should go back on the meds . . . and that I might be
destined to become Pfizer's in-house songwriter. Could
be extremely profitable. But I'll need a chorus . . .

Maybe when meds take your edge away, it makes you
    complacent,
but see my edge is serrated and highly persuasive
like a Cutco knife salesman, bent on slicing my face skin,
so my meds just keep my edge from tryin' to cut my-
    self shaving.

Having milked my med holiday for manic creative exuberance, I know it's time now to go back on the pills. Luckily, they're right where I left them . . . on the floor by the bed.

So what do you think happens after I go back on the meds? I feel better for a while. My friends tell me I seem better. Especially that Deirdre. But then one day, I'm feeling crappy. You can see where this is going . . .

Wait, stop, surely there's no way someone would make the same mistake again, right? After seeing what cold turkey does?

But this is the way the depressed mind works. We always swear it will be different this time. No Adderall to help keep us up. *Just me. Just me and yoga. Just me and meditation.*

Alas, in only a few days I was back at my psychiatrist's office, after suffering a traumatic anxiety attack in Grand Central Station. She recommended not only a return to the old meds but blending in a new med to see if it might be more effective.

I scoffed and shook my head. Another medication? What is this, number three, four? My purse already rattles like a damn maraca everywhere I go. What the fuck. Pitiful. People who need pills are pitiful.

Dr. Innes then pointed out that weeping on the floor of Grand Central sounds pitiful.

It's a clever point, and I couldn't help but be impressed.

Also, I knew I would never get that songwriting deal with Big Pharma if I wasn't an active customer.

The moral of this chapter, and it's an important one to leave you with, is to get used to the prescription life. Staying on your meds, once you decide to, isn't that hard in itself. Popping a pill is one of the easier tasks in life, although I do think the caps could be manufactured to come off with more ease. Just make it easy enough for a child, and I'll find the whole process perfectly luxurious.

The real challenge is this: refilling of a prescription. It's ridiculous that the medical establishment expects the depressed to show up on a monthly basis anywhere, much less at a brightly lit pharmacy where families are loading up on toilet paper and Wiffle Balls.

In general, I think the pharmaceutical experience should vary depending on an individual's physical and psychological situation. Should the contagious really be using the same touch-screen credit card payment device as the rest of us?

If you don't call a pharmacy ahead—and who has the will to think "ahead"?—you will be made to wait for twenty minutes while the pharmacist fills your scrip.

Over the years, I've become quite a pharmacy aficionado. The good news is there is plenty of fun to be had at the pharmacy. I like the pharmacy at Target because the pills come in red bottles and you can get a coffee and explore the whole store while you wait. But even the dullest pharmacy can be fun for twenty minutes.

When I'm browsing in the store, I try to find products that will give me "a new lease on life." Even some small, boring, or mundane product might be enough to give temporary hope of betterment to a depressive.

Eventually, however, you learn that this is always a false hope—and then you can actually relax and enjoy the diversion of walking the aisles without later having an emotional crash when you discover that a brightly colored iPhone case didn't "change everything."

Some people head to a pharmacy with an ailment and look for the best product to treat it. I prefer to look for a product that sounds fun and then generate the ailment it demands. If you're not in the mood to will yourself a hemorrhoid, then you simply look for improvement products. Who doesn't want softer feet or harder feet? Whichever direction you're looking to go, there's a product looking to help you.

You probably do have a lot of legitimate or semi-legitimate ailments, but even if you don't, I want you to understand this advice still applies to you.

Get used to the prescription life.

CONCLUSION:
OFF YOU GO, THEN!

Off you go, then!

Kidding, kidding. No pressure to go anywhere, of course. This is the point at which I invite you to return to the beginning of the book, because really there is no beginning or end to one's depressed hell ... or in our case, this book.

I've ingeniously designed this book to be comforting the whole way through, no matter how many times you've read it. In fact, the book will only get better with every reading, because as you become more familiar with the words, you'll have to do less work to understand them. My literary voice won't be so jarring.

If you are in the mood to "finish a book" in the traditional sense, go ahead and put this book aside for a while. Read something else. Or don't! I understand the desire to celebrate what might be your most traditional achievement in recent memory.

I mean, you read a book! That's something that functionals do. Some people even read books on vacation—so frequently, in fact, that these "beach reads" even have their own fancy moniker.

Point is, you have successfully executed a leisure activity. Don't worry, I'm not about to suggest that you try to "build on your success" and go take up tennis or listen to music. You deserve a rest.

Now if you are reading this page prematurely, having skimmed things a bit, maybe skipped over some chapters, that's good news, too. That's also something the functionals do all the time. They love to save time by assessing potential reading materials, because they have "other things to do."

I have to admit, I'm quite pleased with myself for arriving at this concluding chapter. I wrote a book. I'm feeling cheerier than usual.

If you're thinking of writing a book about depression, I don't want you feeling discouraged because I have clearly stolen the opportunity out from under you. While this book is surely unparalleled in its genius (again, I'm feeling cheerier than usual), I'm sure that you, too, have something to offer, even to this very genre. While you might not know what it is, I am confident it is there. You just need to have faith, okay?

Which leads me to my next point. Have you ever heard of a little something called the Church of Latter-day Saints?

Can you imagine if this *whole thing* was a long con bait-and-switch to get you to join a church?

That would be terrible . . . which is why I'm not asking you to join anything, but just to come along to a sing-along this Wednesday evening. Peter will bring his acoustic and his love of the "strange beauty" of existence.

Now is when I'd like to extend my thanks to you for spending this time with me. Sometimes, your imagined existence comforted me. At other times it annoyed me, sure, when I felt like I was pulling a lot of the weight around here.

Anyway, see you back on page one . . . very soon, I hope. After all, I haven't helped you. You are no more prepared now to face the world. All I offered is company, and my continued company, which is available on . . . page one.

In that way, because this book gave you nothing, it is the book that keeps on giving. It will never stop giving you nothing. This book is like one of those eternal flame memorials. You're *welcome*.

If you want it both ways—to feel the satisfaction of having completed this book, but also want to read it again—please consider picking up a new copy. And maybe one to keep on hand to, say, drop in the lap of the woman weeping in the vibrating pedicure chair next to yours. Yes, her shoulders are shaking from the mechanical shiatsu, but also from her sobs. Not a bad method of camouflage. She might have something to teach you.

Okay, so head to the introduction for your "Hello, again."

Okay, bye, for now.

Hmmm.

Okay, but what about *me*?

I can't very well go back to page one and type the thing again.

I'm feeling like I'm being shoved prematurely out into the world! Once again, you readers make out like bandits, and I am utterly put upon. It's astonishing how much more work I've had to put into this than you did.

Well, I suppose I should think about what's next for me. Breakfast sounds like a reasonable goal. Yes, I'll be going now to order some celebratory nachos for a nice four p.m. breakfast, because I make the rules. I will use an immense and gorgeous teal plastic storage container from Target as my coffee table. Functional people eat dinner on their coffee tables all the time. The plastic tub is substantially weighty, because it is filled with a Santa-worthy heap of unopened mail, none of which I will be facing today.

The depresso way, something I learned by necessity during depression, has left me with a perspective, a free-dom, that enriches the life I live now, now that I'm doing better. For example, the other day the electricity spon-taneously turned off, completely out of nowhere, after six months of my not paying Con Ed. I didn't freak out at all, because I know, the depresso really knows, that it simply does not matter. Sure, I had to pay the fee for turning it back on, but I don't have to perform a shame play about it for myself, the gods, my boyfriend, and the cats, or the sales rep on the Con Ed phone tree. I know intimately how to berate myself, and I certainly don't have time to do it over uninteresting issues like utilities, which . . . let's get real, should be free anyway.

I used to see any such failures as signs of the depression wreaking havoc, and then I'd allow those failures to further depress me. But I know I'm not depressed today, at all. I've definitely been feeling decent for quite some time. I haven't changed my meds in years. I don't think I've been facedown on the floor, in the bad way, of my current apartment even once. The depresso patterns of behavior feel more like a skill at this point, giving me wisdom, like knowing not to use up energy over meaningless things.

Depression burns the mental house to the ground, from deep within its foundation. It destroys all the old ways of looking at things, many of which used to keep you upright, others that were only an incidental part of your home. Depression takes out the structural beams first, weakening them, and then everything collapses around it. The doodads and paintings melting off the walls, the front door cracking and buckling: these are the perspectives you inherited from your family, ideas from society. By society, I, of course, mean television. The forts you fanatically constructed in the wake of childhood traumas, coping mechanisms that no longer serve as cozy nooks. But what this all means is that later, when the depression lifts, when you do have the energy to rebuild a life, you get to start completely fresh. You lay every brick, if you decide you like bricks. Maybe you're into geodesic domes.

I'm not yet sure of how I intend to rebuild. I'm enjoying the open space for now, sleeping under the stars. I know I have a much looser attachment to ideas, and habits, and less sense of propriety than ever before. Yes, I might choose to reinstate in my mind a belief that a modern yet warm fine wood coffee table equals wellness. I might not. It's quite exciting. Kind of like being hit by an arsonist but realizing the old home was crap anyway.

Assuming you are firmly in the muck at the moment, I only want to point out that from where I stand, you're even more okay that you realize. In fact, the more "pathetic" your life is at the moment, the more structures you have undoubtedly burned. The worse it is right now, the more unsullied a hunk of land you'll end up with in the end.

Of course, if this sentiment applies to you at the moment, then you are by definition incapable of finding comfort in it right now, and that's, of course, okay.

In fact, I promised I wouldn't try to make you feel better. I doubt I did.

If you are feeling any better, please note, I will not be held liable.

ACKNOWLEDGMENTS

Thank you so much to all of my family and friends, especially:

My parents, Naomi and Greg Novak, for their patience and love, and my siblings, Rebecca Novak and Jeffrey Novak, for their belief in me.

Chris Laker, who was rarely more than twenty feet away during the writing of this book.

Lauren Oliver, aka Lou, for giving me liftoff and then keeping me in the air. May the world know you not only for your brains but for your looks.

A big thank-you to Foundry Literary + Media, especially the best agent ever, Anthony Mattero, and the entire incredible team at Crown Archetype (especially Suzanne O'Neill, Jenni Zellner, and Jesse Aylen).

Thank you to Mark Chait for your swift assistance during dark days.

Thank you to Dr. Innes, too.

And Snook.

ABOUT THE AUTHOR

Jacqueline Novak is a stand-up comedian who has been featured at comedy festivals across the United States. Her comedy album, *Quality Notions*, is available online. Novak lives in New York.